COFFEE·CUISINE·CONVERSATION

Brown & Rosie

COFFEE·CUISINE·CONVERSATION

FRESH
AND
SIMPLE

Leyli Mustafaeva and Rena Lavery

UNICORN

CONTENTS

6 OUR STORY

9 KEY INGREDIENTS

20 KITCHEN ESSENTIALS

20 FRESH AND FRUITY BREAKFAST

44 BREAKFAST AND BRUNCH

72 SOUPS AND SALADS

112 BIG LUNCHES AND LAZY WEEKENDS

162 LUNCH ON THE GO

186 DESSERTS

220 FROM THE BAKERY

236 JUICES AND SMOOTHIES

251 INDEX

OUR STORY

Our love for food started from a very early age and for as long as we can remember we've enjoyed good cooking, fresh ingredients and interesting flavours.

Our family was always very heavily involved in all aspects of good food, meaning they were very experimental with flavours, not afraid of mixing lots of different spices and fresh herbs to broaden our palates and create exciting new dishes for us kids to get used to.

As young children we watched our aunt in the kitchen, cooking with produce from across the world and experimenting with unusual ingredients. We too were encouraged to experiment, searching through numerous cookbooks for exciting recipes to test our new-found culinary skills. Slowly we became more daring, creating our own innovative flavour combinations.

. . .

Leyli's story

When Leyli moved to Australia, she was amazed by the diversity of Australian cuisine. The hybrid culture and abundance of rare and unusual ingredients meant food was naturally very experimental and innovative. Exciting combinations such as French and English classics infused with Asian ginger and spices inspired her to create new culinary ideas, many of which feature in this book.

She was brought up to enjoy fresh, simple and light food that boosts your energy. Cooking dishes with different ingredients and seasonings can become unlimited and experimental, and the Australian culinary scene has inspired her to create a collection of exciting recipes that are fresh and straighforward to make at home.

Rena's story

Rena loves to revitalise her traditional family recipes with new twists and flavours. Taking inspiration from her travels around Europe, Asia and Africa, she combines comforting childhood favourites with new ingredients and techniques she discovered whilst living and working across the world. Most of her recipes are tried and tested, cooked for her family on a daily basis and based on a great foundation of food. Her dishes are straightforward to make but pack a punch when it comes to seasoning and spice.

. . .

The philosophy behind Brown and Rosie's cafe is simple – to serve food that is good for you, tastes good and makes you feel good.

For our cookbook *Fresh and Simple* we have brought together over one hundred recipes to cook at home, combining our favourite dishes from the café menu with a homemade cooking style that inspires experimentation with taste and presentation. We have simplified tricky techniques and minimised fussy ingredient lists, giving our dishes a modern twist that's still achievable with our busy lives.

The cookbook features recipes for all occasions and meal times, from early morning poached eggs to delicious soups for chilly afternoons or salads for those summer days; from hearty dinners and indulgent desserts to feed the family to juices and smoothies for when you want that all important health kick.

Discover new flavours and ingredients – from traditional boiled eggs with a twist of beetroot spread to soft baked eggs with kale and chorizo; baked salmon fillets to black pepper crab with ginger; from redcurrant muffins to mixed berry pie.

By using the best seasonal produce we are able to create healthy, nutritious dishes that are full of flavour. Our philosophy to support local businesses and suppliers has enabled us to personally meet the farmers and manufacturers, and visit orchards, vineyards, paddocks, fish farms and even an apiary to truly see where food originally comes from.

In essence our book shows our love for an adventurous and wholesome food culture. Inspired by modern global cuisine, *Fresh and Simple* offers the freedom to create exciting, energy boosting dishes that are delicious and easy to make at home.

KEY INGREDIENTS

Eggs

Not only are eggs among the most nutritious foods on the planet, packed full of protein, iodine, vitamins and minerals, they are also the ultimate versatile convenience food. In the art and science of cooking, eggs play an important part in binding other ingredients together, which is especially important in baking. Over the years they have become a breakfast staple and have come back into fashion now we know that their health benefits vastly outweigh their cholesterol level. These are just some of the reasons we love eggs so much and why they are the basis for a lot of our favourite breakfast and brunch dishes.

Nuts and Seeds

There are over fifty nuts that we humans can consume, each one with something slightly different to offer. We love almonds, brazils, peanuts, walnuts, pistachios, cashews and chestnuts. Together with their first cousins, those super seeds, they are great way to add a little bit of crunch to a dish, as well as giving you a quick nutritional fix. No longer just for birds!

Almonds – these little calcium-rich bullets of deliciousness and are also high in Vitamin E, which helps to promote healthy bones and skin. They are also easily blitzed with water to make a dairy-free alternative to milk. If you want to help keep your heart in check opt for whole skin on your almonds, as the skin is full of heart-protecting compounds called flavonoids.

Brazil nuts – these great if you have a low thyroid function, as they are a prime source of selenium which we need to produce the active thyroid hormone. Selenium is also key to supporting our immune systems and helping wounds to heal quickly. It only takes 3 or 4 brazil nuts each day to get your RDA of selenium.

Chestnuts – we all know that nuts have a high fat content of the unsaturated kind, but chestnuts are the nuts with the lowest fat and calorie content and are also rich in starchy carbs and fibre. In their raw form they are a great source of vitamin C but be aware that this drops by about forty per cent after heating. They are lower in protein than other nuts but make a useful contribution of B vitamins, including B6. Ground chestnut flour can be used as a gluten-free flour for cakes and bakes or roast for a tasty, warming snack.

Nigella seeds – also known as black cumin seeds, these have been made famous lately due to their unique source of thymoquinone – a plant chemical that is thought to have potential powers in reducing mutant cell reproduction.

KEY INGREDIENTS

Nigella seeds may also reduce histamine production as well as helping to reduce the power of parasites in the mouth and gut. With a whole range of scientific research studies now proving their worth, no wonder they are becoming a popular choice among the health conscious.

Chia seeds – these nutrient dense seeds are a rich source of Omega-3 fatty acids and the B vitamins thiamine and niacin. We find them a very versatile ingredient that can be easily incorporated into a recipe. When prepared properly, they are easy to digest and provide a great energy boost.

Pulses

Beans and lentils such as borlotti beans, kidney beans, chickpeas and puy lentils are back in fashion after years of just being something our vegan friends ate. The beauty of them is that they are highly nutritious, a great source of protein and very versatile. Furthermore, we now understand that even if vegetarianism is not for you, a couple of meat-free days a week are not only beneficial to the body but also to the planet. Their versatility means that they can be used in many different savoury and sweet dishes; from soups and stews to curries and salads, there's a pulse for every occasion.

We like to cook our beans and lentils from scratch. Dried varieties of beans and pulses will require soaking overnight to remove impurities that can make them difficult to digest, but lentils can just be added to your dish dry and will then soak up the stock or sauce. However, canned varieties of all pulses are a great speedy alternative for a mid-week supper, even if they don't absorb the flavours of the dish quite so deliciously as dried beans.

Oils and Fats

For cooking, a standard olive oil works perfectly well but choose your cooking oil based on what you are making, as different fats and oils work better with different ingredients and processes. If you need to cook something at a high temperature (using a high smoke point) then choose animal fats or olive oil over oils such as corn and sunflower. This is because these vegetable oils are quite unstable at high temperatures and produce aldehydes which can be toxic, leading to an increased risk of heart disease and cancers. Saturated and mono-unsaturated fats such as duck fat, lard and olive oil are much more stable at high temperatures and produce a lot less aldehydes. Keep all oils in a cupboard and try not to reheat them.

Extra virgin olive oil – this is unbeatably delicious, especially in Mediterranean dishes.

KEY INGREDIENTS

As recent studies have shown, there is a link between olive oil and a decreased risk of heart disease, cognitive decline and breast cancer. Olive oil gets its 'extra virgin' status when it is considered unrefined, not treated with any chemicals or altered by temperature. The oil is assessed on three criteria – fruitiness, bitterness and pepperiness. The flavour, smell and colour can vary radically between olive oils, in the same way wines taste vary depending on the grape and where it is produced. There are an array of olive oils on the market but as an oil for salad dressing and marinades we would choose an extra virgin olive oil every time. Choose one that is dark and rich in flavour.

Coconut oil – the extra virgin olive oil of this decade, it is now available everywhere. It has a strong coconut flavour and makes a great alternative to butter in both sweet and savoury recipes, such as honey-baked granola or roasted asparagus omelette.

Sesame oil – this is an edible vegetable oil derived from sesame seeds and is another oil rich in antioxidants. A few drops is all that is needed to bring out its potent flavour, making it a delicious addition to salad dressings. Drizzled on a vegetable soup or tossed through some Chinese noodles, sesame oil will give your dish a very distinctive oriental, nutty flavour.

Flaxseed oil – also known as linseed oil, this contains high omega-3 to omega-6 ratio (see below). It is best used over salads as the dressing or drizzled over stews and soups.

Omega oils are needed now more than ever before, best in the ratio 1:1 Omega-3 to Omega-6. We have too much Omega-6 in our bodies and not enough 3. Balance this by eating oily fish or taking an Omega-3 supplement.

Herbs and Other Seasonings

Herbs are a very concentrated source of flavour and nutrition, with a little going a long way. We like to try and use fresh herbs whenever possible and even better if they have been grown at home.

Herbs are usually best prepared by picking the leaves from the stalks, then chopping them as finely as desired with a chef's knife or two-handled rocking knife (mezzaluna); alternatively, cut bunches of tender herbs such as chives into small pieces using kitchen scissors. Some tender herbs – particularly basil, tarragon and mint – bruise easily, a problem exacerbated by blunt kitchen knives. To prevent bruising and discolouration, avoid chopping these herbs finely; instead, try adding the whole leaves to dishes, or tear them into small pieces with your

KEY INGREDIENTS

fingers. Another great way to use them is as a bouquet garni (a bundle of herbs tied together with string). This is an intense way of flavouring sauces, soups and stews.

The volatile oils that give flavour and fragrance to tender herbs dissipate quickly after exposure to heat, so it's best to add these herbs to dishes towards the end of cooking or just before serving. However, more robust herbs such as bay, sage, rosemary and common thyme are at their best when given time to blend with the other ingredients in the dish, so should be added earlier in the cooking process. Tender herbs – such as basil, chervil, chives, coriander, dill, mint, parsley, tarragon – can also be used raw and make delicious salad ingredients.

Basil – this versatile and widely used aromatic herb is an annual plant that is easy to grow from seed but is sensitive to cold. It grows well in warm climates and is widely used throughout southern Europe, particularly the Mediterranean, and in many parts of Asia. Basil can easily be grown on a kitchen window sill and there is nothing better than a salad of mozzarella and tomato, layered with whole basil leaves and finished with a good glug of olive oil!

Parsley – this multi-purpose herb can be used as a garnish and flavouring and as a vegetable, so should always be kept in plentiful supply. There

are two main varieties: curly-leaf and flat-leaf. Both can be used interchangeably, although flat-leaf parsley has a stronger flavour.

Coriander – even though its name comes from the Greek *koris* meaning bed bug, coriander is one of the world's most commonly used herbs; and in our eyes one of the most delicious! A great source of iron and magnesium, it is green, leafy and strong smelling with a fresh, citrus taste that makes it an invaluable garnish and flavour enhancer. Both the fresh leaves and stalks are edible, as well as the berries, which are dried and called coriander seeds.

Thyme – no kitchen should be without the heady, aromatic taste of thyme. There are many different varieties, both cultivated and wild, with flavours of mint, caraway, lemon and stronger varieties that taste more akin to oregano. It also contains an oil that some people believe protects brain cells against age-related changes.

Dill – also known as dill weed, dill is a green herb with wiry, thread-like leaves that grow in clusters. It has a strong, distinctive taste that is like a combination of fennel, anise and celery, with warm, slightly bitter undertones.

Mint – Pimm's and mojitos aside, mint is of course a great herb to have in your kitchen. It is so easy to grow that you will probably be more

KEY INGREDIENTS

concerned with its abundance than its scarcity. Partner it with watermelon and feta to create a delicious summer salad, infuse it in some hot water for a detoxifying tea, or cook with potatoes to liven them up a bit.

Rosemary – this robust and versatile herb has a flavour that complements a wide variety of dishes and ingredients. Its bittersweet green leaves resemble pine needles. The plant is an evergreen shrub, so the leaves are available fresh all year round and it is a simple one to grow, even on a balcony.

Cayenne – this is a red, hot chilli pepper from the Capsicum genus, packed full of nutritious goodness. However, because we consume it in such small amounts, it actually makes a negligible contribution to our overall dietary intake of nutrients. Its ability to dilate the blood vessels helps speed up the body's metabolism and this in turn can aid weight-loss.

Star Anise – the dominant flavour in Chinese five-spice and also the Indian mixed-spice garam masala, this exotic spice's flavour closely resembles anise with an aroma similar to liquorice. Use it in pho style Vietnamese dishes and try it as part of a marinade for barbequed duck. For something a little different, try roasting some sweet potatoes and ginger for a real taste sensation!

Sumac – this is a tangy, lemony spice often used in Mediterranean and Middle Eastern cooking. Ground down to a powder from the dried berries of the sumac bush that is native to the Middle East, this spice has become more popular over the last few years and is now widely available in supermarkets. Try using it in salads instead of lemon juice or to season grilled meat and fish. It's also delicious sprinkled over hummus.

Cardamom – this contains an essential oil that is believed to fight inflammation and cancer. Best used whole, or at least mashed in a pestle and mortar, cardamom is delicious in curries, as well as in sweet dishes such as baked banana.

Ginger – food is never dull when it contains this root that comes from the same family as cardamom and turmeric. Just as delicious raw as it is cooked, it also has a long history of medicinal uses that date back thousands of years. The magic ingredient is gingerol, the anti-inflammatory compound that gives this root its flavour. It can help prevent flatulence, calm the bowels and help stop nausea and vomiting. Gingerols help protect against cancer, particularly bowel cancer, as well as boosting immune function and helping to fight infection.

KEY INGREDIENTS

Nutrient-Rich Ingredients

There's no magic potion or on-trend fad that is going to guarantee a healthy body and mind, but there are definitely foods to avoid and more importantly foods that give our bodies nourishment in the simplest form. We feel that the essence of keeping the body healthy through food is good old-fashioned balance, keeping ingredients as natural as possible and wherever possible, avoiding processed foods with additives and preservatives. There are great ways you can help your body do the best job possible. The following nutrient-rich foods can help boost the quality of your diet.

Barberries – an important ingredient in Persian cookery, these little red berries bring vibrancy of colour and tartness of flavour to dishes, as well as being high in antioxidants.

Acai berries – these contain called anthocyanins and flavonoids, which give them a higher antioxidant capacity compared to other berries such as raspberries and cranberries. As acai berries have to be frozen within an hour of picking, they are quite expensive, but using an acai powder as an addition to breakfast is a great option.

Kiwi – this fruit is naturally high in vitamins C and K that promote healthy skin and improve immune system performance and cardiovascular health. Kiwis are also a great source of fibre.

Avocado – known as 'nature's butter', avocados are as delicious mashed into a spread as they are as an accompaniment to poached eggs. They contain healthy fats as well as dietary fibre and also act as a nutrient booster, helping the body absorb more fat-soluble nutrients such as alpha and beta-carotene.

Coconut – eaten raw, this offers a spectrum of benefits to nourish your body while delighting your tongue. Rich in fibre, coconut can boost health by normalising bowel movements, reducing the risk of haemorrhoids, preventing blood sugar swings, lowering blood pressure, providing long-lasting satiation that discourages overeating, protecting against diabetes and even boosting your immune system.

Maca powder – grown in Peru, this is produced from the malty-tasting root of the Maca plant and it has been consumed for thousands of years. Maca is most commonly available in powder form and has traditionally been used to improve energy and stamina.

Physalis, or golden berry – these resemble a golden raisin but with a flavour that's more sweet and tart. Physalis contain linoleic and oleic acid, two essential fatty acids that aid in

KEY INGREDIENTS

insulin sensitivity and fat oxidation. We love using them in baking as well as for a delicious fruity snack.

Natural Sweeteners

Dates – these are sweet and rich with a chewy, sticky texture. Fresh dates are plump and dark brown with a glossy sheen. Dried dates look very similar and it can be hard to tell the difference if you buy them packaged. Dried dates are often coated in syrup to keep them soft and sticky. Medjool dates are a popular choice for baking and even though they are a calorific carbohydrate, they are a great source of fibre and B vitamins.

Honey – a naturally sweet, viscous liquid made from the nectar of flowers and collected by bees, honey comes in numerous varieties with different colours, textures and flavours. The flavour, colour and sweetness of honey depends on which type of flower the nectar was collected from. If you suffer from seasonal allergies it is worth trying to use local honey to where you live, as this can help keep hayfever at bay.

Dried fruits – sulphur dioxide is often used as a preservative to keep dried fruit brightly coloured. We tend to use ones which are labelled sulphur dioxide-free. We love using prunes in our dishes. Prunes and plums contain high levels of phytonutrients called phenols. They're particularly high in two unique phytonutrients: neochlorogenic and chlorogenic acid. Numerous studies show that these phytonutrients help to prevent damage to cells particularly when it comes to the oxidation of lipid molecules in the body.

Fresh fruits and berries – who doesn't love fresh fruit? Nature's sweet. We use them to sweeten and enhance the flavour of other foods. We love passionfruit, feijoa, blueberries, cranberries, redcurrants and bilberries. Passionfruit is our most favourite – a rich source of antioxidants, minerals, vitamins, and fibre. One hundred grams of the fruit contains about 97 calories and is just delicious!

Feijoa – also known as pineapple guava or guavasteen, the feijoa is a small tree resembling a shrub. The fruit is sweet-sour in taste and makes a great alternative addition to yogurts, shakes and ice creams. It contains an array of minerals including copper, iron, manganese, calcium, magnesium, phosphorus, and zinc that help ensure your good health. Adding feijoa to your daily diet helps enhance your immunity to a great extent. High amounts of vitamin C, antioxidants and other vital nutrients in the fruit help keep you fit and healthy.

KITCHEN ESSENTIALS

Food Processor

This is one of our essential appliances. Grate a mountain of cauliflower or broccoli into rice in minutes or use as a super-speedy way of making slaws, cakes or cookies. When time is of the essence, why not let a food processor do the hard work for you? We use Magimix but KitchenAid and Kenwood also produce high quality products.

Blender

We use super-powerful blenders that make light work of milk and flour. Our favourite brand if Vitamix. They are so powerful and definitely worth the investment for making the silkiest, creamiest smoothies. They can also handle absolutely anything that you throw into the mix; great for making soups, dips, salsas and everything in between.

Juicer

The slow grinding action of a masticating juicer (also called a cold press juicer) ensure that more of the goodness from the fruits and vegetables makes it into your drinks. You can also use the leftover pulp to make delicious cakes and breads.

Centrifugal juicers do have their merits as they faster, cheaper and easier to clean. The great thing, however, about high-end masticating juicers is that they can also grind coffee, press pasta and make nut butters as well as much more. One of our favourites is the Omega 8004 Juicer, Nutrition Centre.

Sieve

To make your own yogurt or oat milk, you will also need a sieve. In contrast to the above gadgets, a simple stainless steel one is more than adequate.

FRESH AND FRUITY BREAKFAST

FRESH AND FRUITY BREAKFAST

When it comes to weekday mornings, a little bit of citrus zing or berry sweetness can make or break your early start. While there's plenty of sweet bakes and hearty egg dishes to choose from, our regulars often tell us it's the fresh and fruity options that pull them in on their way to the office. From honey-baked granola with dried mango, goji berries and thick, creamy yoghurt to poached spiced quince, we like to think we make it a treat to pack in a few of your five-a-day.

We love to use honey as a sweetener in our breakfast recipes and stock a variety in Rosie's pantry. Manuka, orange-blossom or lavender honey with their luscious fragrance are perfect in this light, creamy porridge. Make it the night before to grab on the way to the front door in the morning.

BIRCHER MUESLI
WITH SEASONAL FRUITS AND PECANS

100g jumbo rolled oats

3 tbsp chia seeds

300ml natural yoghurt

50ml skimmed milk

40g desiccated coconut

100g blueberries

1 passionfruit

½ kiwi fruit, peeled and sliced

½ plum, thinly sliced

4 raspberries

1 tbsp honey

Small handful of toasted coconut flakes

50g pecans

SERVES 2

Put the oats, chia seeds, yoghurt, milk and coconut in a bowl and stir together to combine. Cover then chill in the fridge overnight.

The next morning, stir the fruit through the mix and divide between two bowls. Then drizzle over some honey and sprinkle with toasted coconut flakes and pecans.

This is our basic granola recipe but try out different mixes of dried fruits, nuts and seeds according to taste or what's in the pantry. This version is fabulous, studded with chunks of mango, jewel-coloured goji berries and delicate slivers of almonds, but if you want to get creative, try dried figs, raisins and toasted hazelnuts, or linseeds, sunflower seeds and dried cranberries. A blend of maple syrup and honey is also good.

HONEY-BAKED GRANOLA
WITH ALMOND FLAKES, DRIED MANGO AND GOJI BERRIES

1 tbsp melted coconut oil or extra virgin olive oil

4 tbsp wildflower honey

1 tbsp maple syrup

400g rolled oats

90g flaked almonds

75g sunflower seeds

90g sultanas

50g goji berries

75g dried mango, chopped

1 tsp chia seeds

SERVES 6–8

Preheat the oven to 180°C/350°F/gas mark 4. In a mixing bowl, combine together the oil, honey and maple syrup Add the oats, almonds and sunflower seeds to the bowl and stir until well combined and coated in the honey mix.

Line a baking tray with baking paper then spread out the oat mixture. Bake for 20 minutes until a light golden colour, then turn the tray around in the oven and bake for another 15 minutes until it becomes crisp and a darker golden-brown.

Allow to cool completely; if it hardens and goes crunchy then it is ready, if it is still chewy when cold, you can return it to the oven to bake for a little longer.

Once cooked, tip the granola into a mixing bowl, breaking up any larger chunks with a wooden spoon, then stir through the dried fruit and chia seeds. Store it in an airtight container; it should keep for a couple of weeks, if it lasts that long!

This is the ultimate breakfast on the go. The overnight soak does require a little planning, but really, how hard is it to mix a little coconut milk with chia before bed? You can vary the fruit topping, or even top with a spoonful of jam if you are running short of time in the morning.

COCONUT CHIA PUDDING

50g chia seeds

225ml coconut milk

½ tbsp honey

100g blueberries and raspberries, plus a few to serve.

1 nectarine, peeled and segmented

¼ mango, peeled and cut into slim wedges

Granola, to serve (optional)

SERVES 1

Mix the chia seeds, coconut milk and honey together in glass mason jar or airtight container, then chill for at least 8 hours until the seeds have swelled and thickened.

When ready to eat, spoon the chia mixture into a glass tumbler. Blitz the berries in a blender or with a stick blender then spoon over the pudding. Repeat with the nectarine and mango.

Top with more berries and a sprinkling of granola, and serve.

Glorious fresh quinces with their delicately scented, melt-in-the-mouth flesh are a wonderful winter treat and we love to serve them for breakfast. They can be made in advance and stored in the fridge, although we think they're best served at room temperature so, if you have time, take them out of the fridge at least half an hour before serving.

POACHED SPICED QUINCE

1 strip of lemon peel and juice of ½ lemon

200g brown sugar

1 good quality chamomile tea bag

750ml water

6 small quinces, peeled, cored and quartered

SERVES 4

Put the lemon peel, brown sugar, tea bag and water in a saucepan and heat gently, stirring occasionally until the sugar has dissolved completely, around 3-4 minutes.

Bring the liquid to the boil and add the quinces. Then reduce the heat and simmer for 45-60 minutes until the quinces are tender and a deep pinkish-red, and the liquid is syrupy.

Let the quinces cool in the syrup, then stir in the lemon juice and serve.

These fantastically fluffy pancakes are about as close to sublime as you can get. And oh-so-perfectly-delicious combined with juicy blueberries and super-sweet honey.

FLUFFY PIKELETS
WITH BLUEBERRIES

300g self-raising flour

½ tsp bicarbonate of soda

50g caster sugar

1 egg, beaten lightly

450g buttermilk
or natural yoghurt

Butter or olive oil, for frying

Good-quality honey, to serve

Large handful of blueberries,
to serve

SERVES 4

Sift the flour and bicarbonate of soda together into a medium bowl then stir in the sugar. Make a well in the centre then gradually stir in the egg and enough buttermilk or yoghurt for a smooth, pouring consistency. Let the mixture stand for 15 minutes.

Heat a non-stick frying pan over a medium heat with a little butter. Drop tablespoonfuls of batter – around 3 at a time – into the pan to cook, allowing room for spreading. Cook for 1-2 minutes then, when bubbles begin to appear on the surface of the pikelets, flip them over and cook for a further minute, until golden.

Keep these warm in a low oven whilst you repeat with the rest of the batter. Serve warm with a drizzle of honey and the blueberries.

We've put these in the breakfast chapter, but they work well as an indulgent treat at any other time of day – just add a big scoop of ice cream for a dessert! This recipe requires a waffle maker, but it's a worthwhile investment as there are very few times of day or night when waffles don't seem like a good idea.

BANANA & PEACH WAFFLES
WITH SPICED MAPLE SYRUP

1 peach, stone removed and halved

3 nectarines, stones removed and halved

1 cinnamon stick

2 cloves

2 star anise

3 tbsp honey

250g plain flour, sifted

2 tsp baking powder

50g caster sugar

½ tsp salt

250ml milk

2 eggs

115g butter, melted, plus extra for brushing

3 bananas, peeled and thickly sliced

50g blueberries, for decoration

Maple syrup, to serve

Preheat the oven to 180°C/350°/gas mark 4. Line a roasting tray with baking paper. In a bowl, toss the peach and nectarines with 2 tablespoons of the honey then arrange in a single layer on the tray. Nestle in the cinnamon, cloves and star anise, then roast for 15-20 minutes, until the fruit is tender and just starting to caramelise.

Meanwhile, make the waffle batter. Combine the flour, baking powder, and salt in a large bowl then make a well in the middle. In a separate bowl, whisk together the milk, eggs, sugar and butter, then pour about half into the dry ingredients and begin whisking, adding the rest gradually to make a smooth batter.

Heat the waffle maker, then brush with melted butter and pour in enough batter to fill. Close the lid and cook for about 5 minutes until crisp and golden. Keep the waffles warm on a baking sheet in a low oven while you cook the remaining waffles and prepare the banana.

Heat a griddle pan, brush with some butter. Toss the banana slices with the honey and fry until golden and caramelised, around 5 minutes.

To serve, divide the waffles among four plates, then top with the cooked fruit and blueberries. Drizzle with maple syrup.

SERVES 4

We like to think of this as a cheat's pancake stack, on those weekend mornings when the faff of weighing flour and frying in batches seems a bit too much like hard work. You can adapt the fruit depending on the season; this also works well with apple compote, roasted pears and baked rhubarb.

CHERRIES ON BRIOCHE
WITH BERRY & ELDERFLOWER YOGHURT

200g thick natural yoghurt

2 tbsp elderflower cordial

1 tbsp honey

100g cherries, pitted

100g mixed berries, such as raspberries, blueberries and blackberries

6 slices of brioche loaf, toasted

1 tbsp icing sugar, for dusting

SERVES 2

Place the yoghurt, honey and 1 tablespoon of elderflower cordial in a bowl and stir to combine. In a separate bowl, combine the cherries and berries with the rest of the cordial.

Spread a slice of brioche loaf with thick layer of the yoghurt mixture then top with some of the fruit. Top with another slice of brioche and repeat the process until you have three layers of each ingredient. Dust with icing sugar to serve.

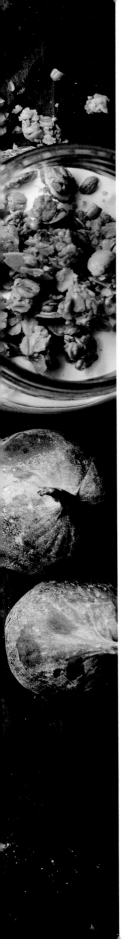

Use black mission figs for this if you can, and the best quality yoghurt you can afford; the taste of these two ingredients will make all the difference and create a real stand-out breakfast dish.

CARAMELISED FIGS
WITH YOGHURT *IN* BREAKFAST JARS

8 figs, washed and halved

1 tbsp maple syrup

2 tbsp pistachios, shelled

1 tbsp desiccated coconut

400ml natural yoghurt

Homemade honey-baked granola, to serve (see page 27)

SERVES 4

Preheat the oven to 190°C/380°F/gas mark 5 and line a baking tray with baking paper. Place the figs on the tray, drizzle with maple syrup and bake for 15 minutes.

Remove the figs from the oven, scatter with the pistachios and sprinkle over the desiccated coconut. Divide the yoghurt between 4 bowls, then top with the figs and a little granola.

Feijoa is a delicious green fruit with a sweet aroma and tangy flavour, reminiscent of pineapple, strawberry and mint. Also known as pineapple guava, it originated in South America but is now popular across the world and usually available in the UK from March to June. Our easy to follow feijoa spread recipe makes the most of its delicious sweet-sour taste and rich vitamin C content – we love in the mornings on our freshly baked sourdough.

FEIJOA SPREAD

1kg feijoas
800g caster sugar

Wash the feijoas and trim off the leafy ends. Place in a blender and blitz for a few seconds to break down the fruit into a coarse pulp, then add the sugar and blend again to mix thoroughly.

Transfer to a bowl and leave until the sugar has completely dissolved and a sweet, sticky spread is formed; this will take a couple of hours.

Meanwhile sterilise the jars and lids by washing them in hot soapy water, rinsing and placing on a baking sheet in the oven at 160°C/280°F/gas mark 1 for 20 minutes or by washing them on a hot dishwasher cycle.

Leave the jars to cool before filling. The spread can be kept in the fridge for up to three months.

Everyone needs a good granola bar recipe up their sleeve for those weeks when breakfast before you leave the house is an impossibility. These are also great after-school snacks for kids.

GRANOLA BARS

200g rolled oats

50g linseeds

100g pumpkin seeds

100g dried cranberries

100g mulberries

8 tbsp honey

MAKES 12 BARS

Preheat the oven to 160°C/325°F/gas mark 3. Line an 18 x 25cm baking tin with baking paper.

Mix the oats, seeds and berries in a large bowl. Heat the honey gently in a pan then pour into the oat mixture and stir to combine.

Press the mixture into the lined baking tin and bake for 20 minutes or until golden brown. Allow to cool in the tin and then slice into 12 bars.

BREAKFAST AND BRUNCH

BREAKFAST AND BRUNCH

A relaxed brunch with friends at the weekend is one of life's greatest pleasures; Saturdays at the café are packed with customers and their families catching up on the week's events, while weekdays see everyone from new mums to local business owners taking some time to fuel the day ahead. Our fresh herbed ricotta with avocado and kumatos is extremely popular in the warmer months, while baked eggs with kale and chorizo can't be beaten on a cold, rainy day. Year-round though, people can't get enough of our dill-cured salmon, especially when it's served with scrambled eggs and seeded rye.

This open sandwich of sorts is is both filling and nourishing when that cold snap in the air arrives. Most wild mushrooms are in season in autumn, with the exception of the morel in spring. Try any combination, such as chanterelle, cep and oyster.

PORTOBELLO MUSHROOMS POACHED EGG AND HUMMUS ON SOURDOUGH

100g broccoli, cut into florets

1 tbsp olive oil

200g wild mushrooms, sliced

Salt

Pinch of crushed dried chilli

4 eggs

4 thick slices sourdough, toasted

50g firm goat's cheese
or feta, crumbled

FOR THE HUMMUS

200g canned chickpeas

½ garlic clove, crushed

Juice of ½ a lemon

1 tbsp tahini

3 tbsp extra virgin olive oil

Salt and ground black pepper

2 tsp dukkah

SERVES 4

First, make the hummus. Put the chickpeas, garlic, lemon juice, tahini, olive oil and a little seasoning in a food processor and blend until smooth. If the mixture is too dry and you're having trouble blending it, add a few more tablespoons of olive oil to help things along. Scoop into a bowl and sprinkle with the dukkah.

Next, steam the broccoli for about 5 minutes until tender, then set aside.

Heat the oil in a large, non-stick frying pan, add the mushrooms and a pinch of salt, and fry for about 5 minutes until just cooked. Add the broccoli, sprinkle over a little crushed dried chilli and toss together until the broccoli is warmed through. Set aside, keeping warm.

To poach the eggs, half-fill a pan with boiling water and bring to the boil. Reduce the heat to a gentle simmer, then crack each egg into a cup and gently slide into the water. Cook for about 2–4 minutes until firm, then remove with a slotted spoon and drain on kitchen paper.

Working quickly, spread a generous layer of hummus on each slice of sourdough toast, spoon on the warm mushroom and broccoli mixture and top with a poached egg. Sprinkle with the cheese and serve.

Inspired by the classic Mexican huevos divorciados, we have created our own simple brunch version. Traditionally the eggs are served on opposite sides of the plate – one coated in salsa roja, the other with salsa verde and 'divorced' with a line of refried beans and tostadas. We like to go for a more loving approach and serve our eggs together, leaving you to combine your eggs, salsa, beans and tortilla as you like.

SOFT-FRIED EGGS
WITH GREEN AND RED SALSA

4 large soft tortillas
1 tbsp extra virgin olive oil,
plus extra to fry the eggs
8 eggs
Refried beans, heated through, to serve

FOR THE GREEN SALSA
2 spring onions, finely chopped
½ green pepper, seeded and finely chopped
¼ fresh Serrano chilli,
seeded and finely chopped
1 tbsp olive oil
2 handfuls of coriander leaves, chopped
Salt

FOR THE RED SALSA
½ jalapeno chilli
½ garlic clove, crushed
4 tomatoes, seeded and finely chopped
½ red pepper, seeded and finely chopped
12 fresh basil leaves, torn
1 tbsp olive oil
Salt

Preheat the oven to 200°C/400°F/gas mark 6. Brush both sides of the tortillas with olive oil and bake for 5–10 minutes, until crisp.

As the tortillas bake, combine together all the green salsa ingredients with a pinch of salt and set aside. Combine together the red salsa ingredients with a pinch of salt and set aside.

Once the tortillas are baked, fry the eggs in plenty of olive oil to your liking.

To serve, on each plate arrange 2 fried eggs, a generous spoonful of refried beans, 2 tortillas and a spoonful of each salsa.

SERVES 4

We love these simple, delicately flavoured fritters; the best thing about them is their versatility – they will suit any meal of the day. We like to eat them in the mornings with a dollop of yoghurt, but for a more substantial brunch, try them with a couple of strips of crispy prosciutto on the side.

COURGETTE FRITTERS
WITH HERBY YOGHURT

2 courgettes, coarsely grated

2 spring onions, finely sliced

2 tbsp roughly chopped dill

3 eggs

2 tbsp plain flour

1 tsp barberries

Salt and ground black pepper

2 lemons – zest and juice of one, the other cut into wedges to serve

Olive oil, for frying

Green leaf salad, to serve

FOR THE HERBED YOGHURT

1 cucumber, deseeded and diced

350g Greek or natural yoghurt

1 tbsp finely chopped dill

1 tbsp finely chopped flat-leaf parsley

SERVES 4

Put the grated courgettes in a sieve lined with kitchen paper. Using a wooden spoon, press out as much water as possible, then wrap up in the paper and give one final squeeze before tipping into a mixing bowl. Stir in the spring onion and dill, then add the eggs, flour and barberries and whisk well. Season and add the lemon zest and juice.

Heat a non-stick frying pan with a generous drizzle of olive oil. Drop spoonfuls of the fritter mix into the pan and fry for around 3–5 minutes on each side until golden and crisp. You'll need to do this batches, keeping the cooked fritters warm in a low oven.

Once all the fritters are cooked, dress each plate with a little green salad and divide the fritters between them. Mix together the ingredients for the yoghurt and top the fritters with a spoonful of this and a lemon wedge on the side.

This recipe is perfect for those who like a real savoury edge to their breakfast. The crunch of the radishes and wonderfully soft flesh of the fish make for a riot of textures that will suit any time of day, though.

SALMON AND FENNEL
WITH HORSERADISH SPREAD

4 slices of dark rye bread
(preferably Danish)

12 slices of cured salmon

5 pink radishes, thinly sliced

1 small fennel bulb,
sliced lengthways, fronds reserved

1 tbsp sesame seeds

1 tbsp nigella seeds

4 pickled cucumbers, sliced

Red caviar, to decorate (optional)

FOR THE HORSERADISH SPREAD

200g crème fraiche

4 tbsp freshly grated horseradish

1 tbsp chopped dill

Zest of 1 small lemon,
plus 2 tbsp juice

Salt and ground pepper

SERVES 4

First make the horseradish spread. In a bowl combine the crème fraiche, horseradish, dill, and the zest and juice of the lemon, then season to taste with salt and pepper.

Spread the horseradish mix on the slices of bread then top with the salmon, radishes, fennel slices, sesame and nigella seeds and pickled cucumber slices. Decorate with a few fennel fronds (and some red caviar if you like) then serve.

When the UK asparagus season begins, all we want to do is lightly roast it and dress it with butter, but for those times when something a little more substantial is required, this omelette ticks all the right boxes. It's so elegant, we've even served it as a starter.

OMELETTE
WITH ROASTED ASPARAGUS

FOR THE OMELETTE
3 free range eggs
1 tsp extra virgin olive oil

FOR THE FILLING
50g asparagus spears
½ tbsp coconut oil, melted
Sea salt and ground black pepper
½ tsp chilli flakes
Juice of ½ a lemon
25g goat's cheese
2 tomatoes, sliced
25g hazelnuts, chopped
1 tsp pumpkin seeds
Handful of mint leaves, chopped

SERVES 2

Preheat oven to 180°C/350°F/gas mark 4. On a baking sheet, brush the asparagus spears with the coconut oil. Season with sea salt, pepper and chilli flakes, then roast the asparagus in the oven for 15–20 minutes, or until just browned.

When the asparagus is ready, remove from the oven and set aside close by, with the other filling ingredients. Break the eggs into a bowl, season well and whisk with a fork. Heat a non-stick frying pan over a high heat and add the olive oil, tilting the pan to coat the entire base.

When the oil is very hot, pour in half of the beaten egg and move the pan back and forth to spread it evenly around. Draw the sides of the omelette into the centre with a spatula so the liquid egg can flow to the edge.

Once the omelette has set but is still soft in the centre (after about a minute of cooking), lay half of the asparagus spears and tomato slices on one side of the omelette. Sprinkle over half of the goats cheese and hazelnuts then fold the omelette in half.

Gently slide the omelette onto a plate, drizzle with lemon juice and scatter over some pumpkin seeds and mint. Serve immediately and then repeat to make a second omelette.

We love to serve spicy chorizo sausage with our soft-baked eggs; in this instance, fresh Spanish chorizo sausage imparts a lovely smoky flavour to the tomato sauce as it cooks.

SOFT-BAKED EGGS
WITH KALE AND CHORIZO

1 tbsp olive oil

½ garlic clove, crushed

½ red chilli, deseeded and chopped

1 red pepper, roughly diced

400g tin chopped tomatoes

Salt and ground black pepper

2 fresh Spanish chorizo sausages, halved lengthways

2 handfuls of shredded kale leaves

4 large eggs

Rye bread, toasted, to serve

SERVES 2

Heat the oil in a frying pan, then add the garlic and chilli and fry gently for 1 minute, until fragrant. Add the red pepper, then cook for 2–3 minutes, until softened a little.

Add the chopped tomatoes to the pan with a little seasoning, then simmer gently for about 15 minutes, stirring occasionally, until the pepper is tender and the sauce thickens.

Preheat the oven to 200°C/400°F/gas mark 6. In a separate frying or griddle pan, cook the chorizo for 3–4 minutes each side, until browned and cooked through.

Divide the tomato sauce between two small ovenproof dishes, or one large one. Using a spoon, create a little hole for each egg, then crack them into them. Nestle the cooked sausages into the sauce beside them, then bake it for 5–8 minutes, until the egg is cooked to your liking.

Once the eggs are in the oven, steam or boil the kale until tender, then serve with the eggs and some toasted rye bread on the side.

You'll need to plan ahead to make our salmon cured in dill as it ideally needs 48 hours in the fridge before it's ready to serve, but that also makes it ideal for lazy weekends. Get it ready on Saturday morning, enjoy your day then it's all good to go for Sunday brunch. Choose a good, even, chunky fillet of salmon and trim off any thinner bits so that the fish cures evenly.

DILL-CURED SALMON

1kg salmon fillet, skin on and pin-boned

250g rock salt, plus extra to serve

3 tsp dill or fennel seeds

Finely grated zest of 2 lemons

2 bunches of dill, leaves and stalks, chopped

SERVES 4

Pat the flesh of the salmon dry with kitchen towel. Put a large piece of cling film in the bottom of a deep roasting tin or glass dish, enough so it hangs over the sides, then lay the salmon skin-side down in it.

Combine the salt, dill seeds and lemon zest then spread the mixture over the fish. Scatter with half of the dill, spreading all the way the edges and pressing firmly. Wrap the fish in the cling film as tightly as you can, then chill for 24 hours, turning the fish over halfway through.

When the curing time is up, scrape off all the curing ingredients, then wipe clean of salt mixture. Scatter over the rest of the dill and a little more salt. To serve, thinly slice salmon on an angle with a long sharp knife, detaching it from the skin.

Smooth, creamy ricotta with its almost crumbly texture is delicious served with herbs, sweet red grapes and intensely flavoured Kumato tomatoes. If you can't find this unusual fruit, try swapping it out for fresh figs.

FRESH HERBED RICOTTA
WITH KUMATO, AVOCADO AND GRAPES

100g ricotta

1 tsp snipped chives

1 tsp chopped tarragon

2 avocados, halved, stone removed and flesh mashed

50g of red grapes

120g Kumato tomatoes, cut into quarters or eighths

4 slices sourdough, toasted

ground black pepper

SERVES 4

Combine the ricotta, chives and tarragon then chill in the fridge. Mix the mashed avocado with the grapes and Kumato tomatoes.

Place a slice of sourdough toast on each plate, Spread the avocado mixture on top, then finish with generous spoonfuls of herbed ricotta.

This is one of those amazing recipes that looks stylish and sophisticated, but is incredibly quick and simple to make. We like it made with white crab meat, piled up high on top of our zesty, herby avocado mix.

CRAB BRUSCHETTA
WITH CRUSHED AVOCADO AND LIME AIOLI

120g white crab meat

Large handful
of fresh rocket leaves

2 avocados, peeled,
stone removed and flesh
roughly crushed with a fork

4 thick slices seeded
sourdough toast, halved

1 tsp black sesame seeds

FOR THE LIME AIOLI

1 garlic clove, finely chopped

Pinch of sea salt

2 egg yolks

Juice of ½ lime

2 tbsp olive oil

SERVES 4

For the lime aioli, mix the garlic, salt and egg yolks in a small bowl. Transfer to a bigger bowl and whisk in the olive oil, a little at a time, until emulsified. Add in most of the lime juice and whisk again, then mix three-quarters of it with the crab meat and rocket.

Mix the avocado with the rest of the lime juice, then place two toast halves on each plate, spoon on the avocado spread and top with spoonfuls of dressed crab. Drizzle over a little more dressing and a sprinkling of toasted black sesame seeds to serve.

Deep-green puy lentils are great for carrying bolder flavours and have a wonderful, firm texture. We love them cooked simply with fresh herbs and lemon juice, then paired with tomatoes, golden baked polenta and poached eggs. Packs of ready-made polenta are available in most supermarkets, but nothing beats making it fresh, then slicing and grilling it like we do at Brown and Rosie's.

HERBED LENTILS
WITH GRILLED POLENTA, ROASTED TOMATOES AND POACHED EGG

200g puy lentils

1 bay leaf

2 tbsp extra virgin olive oil

1 onion, finely diced

2 celery sticks, finely diced

Juice of ½ a lemon

Small handful of flat-leaf parsley, chopped

Sea salt and ground black pepper

4 eggs

4 plum tomatoes, halved

FOR THE POLENTA

500ml water

170g instant polenta

80g Parmesan, finely grated

20g butter, cubed

2 rosemary sprigs, finely chopped

Sea salt and ground black pepper

Olive oil for frying

Natural yoghurt, to serve

First, make the polenta. Prepare a 20cm baking tin with baking paper. Boil the water in a large saucepan then gradually add the polenta, whisking continuously for 2–3 minutes. Remove from the heat and stir through the parmesan, butter, rosemary and a generous amount of salt and pepper, then immediately tip into the baking tin. Allow to cool to room temperature, then chill in the fridge for 1 hour, until firm and set.

Bring a medium-sized saucepan of water to boil and add the lentils and bay leaf. Cook for about 20 minutes until the lentils are tender, then drain and remove the bay leaf. As the lentils cook, heat the oil in a large pan and fry the onions and celery for 5–7 minutes until tender. Combine this with the lentils then squeeze over the lemon juice, season and stir in the parsley. Set aside.

Preheat the oven to 200°C/400°F/gas mark 6, then arrange the tomatoes in a baking dish cut side up, drizzle over a little oil and seasoning and roast for about 15–20 minutes.

When the tomatoes are nearly cooked, fry the polenta. Slice into thick wedges in the tin, then remove. Heat 1cm depth of oil in a large non-stick frying pan over a medium heat, then add the polenta, cooking in batches for 2–3 minutes on each side or until golden. Keep warm in a low oven with the tomatoes.

Once all the elements are ready, poach the eggs. To serve, divide the lentils between four plates, then add a few pieces of the polenta and the roasted tomatoes. Top with a poached egg and a dollop of yoghurt.

SERVES 4

A breakfast as vibrant and colourful as this does more than just add a little more goodness to your diet; the contrasting textures and flavours will leave you feeling much more satisfied than any bacon sandwich could.

OUR HEALTHY BREAKFAST PLATE

4 organic, free range eggs

4 baby carrots, peeled and sliced

2 large handfuls of kale

2 sundried tomatoes, sliced

4 radishes, trimmed

2 balls or spoonfuls of labneh

4 tbsp almond dukkah

1 tbsp olive oil

Seeded crackers, to serve

FOR THE BEETROOT SPREAD

400g raw beetroot, peeled and roughly chopped

1 garlic clove, peeled

1 tbsp tahini

1 tbsp lemon juice

2 tbsp olive oil

SERVES 2

First make the beetroot spread. Boil the beetroot for about 30 minutes, until tender. Once ready, place the beetroot, garlic, tahini and lemon juice into a food processor and blend to a coarse paste. Then, with the food processor on a lower setting, slowly add in the oil and mix until thick and smooth.

Next boil the eggs in simmering water, cooking for 6–8 minutes so the yolk remains runny, then cool immediately under cold running water.

Arrange the carrots, kale, tomato, radishes, beetroot spread and labneh between 2 serving boards or plates. Peel the eggs carefully then roll them in a little oil, followed by dukkah. Lay the eggs in the middle of the board and serve immediately.

SOUPS AND SALADS

SOUPS AND SALADS

Being surrounded by so many thriving local businesses, we know how important it is to have something hearty and healthy on offer at lunchtime, whether it's to eat in or take away. From grain salads with roasted vegetables and creamy goat's cheese to our fragrant butternut squash soup, you can have a meal in minutes to eat back at your desk. But for those times when you need a little headspace, Asian-inspired beef noodle salads with peanuts or even warm roasted cauliflower with tahini dressing provide a good enough reason for a break in the day.

Stracchino is a very young, fresh Italian cheese, with a gorgeously soft texture. If you can't find it, try using a soft, mild goat's cheese, or even mozzarella or burrata.

POACHED CHICKEN
AND
STRACCHINO SALAD

8 boneless, skinless chicken mini-fillets

1 onion, peeled and chopped into wedges

2 celery stalks, roughly chopped

Salt and ground black pepper

1 fennel bulb, trimmed and very finely sliced

1 carrot, peeled and cut into long strips

Handful of watercress

100g sugar snap peas

100g dried cranberries

50g stracchino cheese, roughly chopped

Handful of cashew nuts, toasted

FOR THE LEMON FENNEL SEED DRESSING

1 medium shallot, peeled and finely chopped

1 tsp wholegrain mustard

1 tsp fennel seeds

Zest and juice of 1 lemon

1 tbsp extra virgin, olive oil

Salt and ground black pepper

SERVES 4

Place the chicken in a saucepan with the onion, celery and plenty of seasoning. Cover with water and bring to a boil, then simmer for 15 minutes.

Meanwhile, make the salad. Put the finely sliced fennel, carrot, watercress, sugar snap peas, and cranberries in a bowl, then toss to combine.

Make the dressing by whisking the shallot, mustard, fennel seeds, lemon zest and juice together. Whisk in the oil, then season to taste with salt and pepper.

Drizzle the dressing over the salad and toss to combine. Divide between four plates, then top with the chicken, stracchino cheese and toasted cashew nuts.

*This is the kind of meal that will leave you feeling light,
bright and satisfied. It wouldn't survive a lunchbox,
though, so make this moments before you want to eat it.
It also makes a great starter for six.*

SEARED TUNA SALAD

50g linseeds

1 tsp fennel seeds

120g piece of yellowfin tuna fillet
or sashimi tuna

1–2 tbsp olive oil

1 banana shallot, very thinly sliced

1 carrot, peeled into ribbons

1 chinese radish (mooli), peeled into
ribbons

35g roasted peanuts

2 large handfuls of salad leaves

FOR THE DRESSING

1½ tbsp Chinese sesame seed paste

2 tbsp light soy sauce

1½ tbsp rice wine vinegar

2 garlic cloves, finely chopped

2 tbsp finely grated ginger

2 tbsp sesame oil

To make the dressing mix the sesame paste and soy
sauce in a small bowl. Add in the vinegar and whisk to
combine, then add the garlic, ginger and sesame oil and
allow to stand for 30 minutes so the flavours develop.

Next, prepare the tuna. Spread the linseeds and fennel
seeds out on a tray, then roll the tuna through it, getting
as many seeds as possible to stick to the outside. Place
the oil in a frying pan over a high heat, then sear the
tuna on all sides, about 30 seconds on each, until it has
a cooked edge about 5mm thick, keeping the centre raw.
Remove from the pan, then leave it to cool in the fridge
while you prepare the other ingredients.

Combine the shallots, carrots and mooli in a large bowl.
Add the salad leaves, roasted peanuts and most of the
dressing, then toss together. Divide between four plates,
then thinly slice the tuna and place on top. Add the rest
of the dressing, if you like, then serve.

SERVES 4

This silky smooth soup feels like a little bit of luxury; even better, it's ready in less than 30 minutes. Serve with good quality crusty bread.

WILD MUSHROOM SOUP

2 tbsp olive oil, plus a little extra to serve

1 garlic clove, finely chopped

1 medium leek, thinly sliced

500g wild mushrooms, sliced

500ml water, chicken stock or vegetable stock

60ml double cream, plus extra to serve

Salt and ground black pepper

Handful flat leaf parsley, chopped, to serve

Zest of 1 lemon

SERVES 4

Heat the olive oil in a saucepan over medium heat, then add the garlic, leek and wild mushrooms, reserving a small handful for the topping. Stir continuously until the mushrooms and leeks are just tender, around 5 minutes. Add the stock or water and cook over a low heat for 15–20 minutes, until the leeks are really soft. Add the cream then pour into a blender and blend until smooth. Season to taste.

Towards the end of the cooking time, add a little oil to a frying pan and cook the reserved mushrooms until golden. Remove from the heat, then stir through the parsley and lemon zest.

To serve, ladle the soup into bowls, top with the mushroom and parsley mixture and an extra swirl of cream.

Ceviche sounds much more intimidating to prepare than it really is. Just make sure you buy the best quality, freshest fish. This also works well with salmon fillets.

TUNA CEVICHE ON LETTUCE LEAVES

180g tuna, sashimi quality, finely sliced

1 avocado, peeled, stone removed and sliced

Zest and juice of 1 lime

1 tbsp extra virgin olive oil

Salt and ground black pepper

½ grapefruit, peeled and segmented

50g bean sprouts

1 jalapeño chilli, sliced into rings

Handful coriander leaves

1 tbsp nigella seeds

1 tbsp beetroot sauerkraut (optional)

1 little gem lettuce, leaves separated and washed

Put the tuna and avocado in a shallow bowl, then in a separate bowl, mix together the lime zest and juice, olive oil, salt and pepper. Pour the dressing over the tuna and avocado and gently mix together. Chill in the fridge for 1 hour.

Put the lettuce leaves on a serving platter, then divide the tuna and avocado between the lettuce leaves, followed by the grapefruit, bean sprouts, chilli, coriander leaves and nigella seeds. Top with the beetroot sauerkraut, if using, then roll up and eat. Alternatively, you can serve these as little canapé boats.

SERVES 2–4

Make sure you leave a little crunch in your asparagus for a good contrast with the tender red pepper salad. If you don't have a barbecue, you can cook this in a griddle pan on the hob.

ASPARAGUS AND HALLOUMI SALAD

Olive oil

3 whole red peppers

50g green olives

2 tbsp extra virgin olive oil

1 tbsp white wine vinegar

Salt and ground black pepper

250g block of halloumi, sliced

Small handful of basil leaves

2 bunches asparagus

Crusty bread, to serve

SERVES 4

Heat a barbecue hotplate on medium-high heat, brush with oil then cook the peppers for 10 minutes or until charred on all sides. Transfer to a bowl, cover with cling film and let stand for 5 minutes. Once cool enough to handle, peel the skin, remove the seeds and roughly chop, then place in a bowl with the olives and basil leaves. Whisk the oil, vinegar, salt and pepper in a jug then add to the peppers and olives and toss to combine.

Cook the asparagus on the barbeque plate for 5 minutes until just tender, then cook the halloumi slices until golden. Serve with the red pepper salad and crusty bread.

Black rice is one of our favourite bases for filling and healthy salads, not only for its firm texture and nutty flavour, but for the beautiful contrast it gives to vibrant veg. This can be anything from a packed lunch, a quick evening meal or even a smart but simple starter at the weekend.

BLACK RICE, KALE AND AUBERGINE SALAD

500ml black rice, soaked for 1 hour or more

1 litre water

1 tsp sea salt

3 cardamom pods

FOR THE AUBERGINE

½ tsp pomegranate molasses

Salt and ground black pepper

5 tbsp extra virgin olive oil

4 tbsp lemon juice

1 large aubergine, cut into small cubes

FOR THE SALAD

2 large stems of kale, rib removed and leaves finely chopped

1 tsp lemon juice

1 tbsp olive oil

1 avocado, stone removed and cubed

½ red onion, finely chopped

1 handful fresh mint, leaves picked and chopped

Small handful raw pistachio nuts, coarsely chopped

5 dried apricots, chopped

125ml yoghurt, to serve

Preheat the oven to 200°C/400°F/gas mark 6.
Rinse and drain rice and place in a saucepan with the water, salt and cardamom pods. Cover with a lid and bring to boil. Lower the heat and simmer for about 30 minutes, or until all the water has been absorbed, then allow to cool.

Meanwhile, prepare the aubergine. Mix together the pomegranate molasses, salt, pepper, olive oil and lemon juice. Put the aubergine on a large baking tray, then drizzle over the dressing, tossing to combine. Bake in the oven for about 30 minutes, or until soft on the inside and slightly browned on the outside. Allow to cool.

Place the chopped kale in a medium serving bowl, add lemon juice and olive oil and massage the kale for a couple of minutes until softened. Add the rest of the ingredients, including the rice and aubergine, then toss to combine. Divide between plates then serve with a dollop of yoghurt.

SERVES 4

This dish is for the hottest of summer days – refreshing, sweet and salty in equal measure. We like to serve this alongside a couple of other salads, but it works perfectly well on its own, too.

WATERMELON AND FETA SALAD

1kg watermelon, seeds removed and thinly sliced

100g feta cheese, crumbled

10 sprigs of fresh mint, leaves stripped and torn

10 sprigs of fresh basil, leaves stripped and torn

2 tbsp olive oil

Salt and ground black pepper

SERVES 4

Line up the watermelon slices on a platter. Scatter over the cheese, and herbs. Drizzle with the oil and seasoning, then serve.

We like to make this soup when tomatoes are at their best, then freeze a few portions for those cold winter days when you need a little burst of sunshine.

ROASTED TOMATO SOUP
WITH
SWEET POTATOES

1kg Roma tomatoes, halved

2 tbsp olive oil

3 sprigs fresh thyme

Salt and ground black pepper

400g sweet potatoes, peeled and chopped

2 rosemary sprigs

1 litre water

1 onion, chopped

1 green chilli, seeded and chopped

2 tbsp tomato purée

Handful of fresh basil leaves, to serve

SERVES 4

Preheat to 220°C/440°F/gas mark 7, then place the tomatoes on a baking tray. Drizzle with half the oil and top with thyme. Season well, then roast for 15 minutes, until tender.

At the same time, place the sweet potatoes onto a second baking tray, drizzle with the rest of the olive oil, season and top with the rosemary, then roast for 20 minutes. Set both trays aside to cool a little.

Boil the water with the onion, chilli and a little salt for 10 minutes to make a light vegetable stock. Then pour into a food processor together with the roasted tomatoes and tomato purée, and blend until smooth. Taste for seasoning, then ladle into bowls and top with basil leaves. Serve with the roasted sweet potatoes.

Our lunchtime menu would not be complete without this Middle-Eastern inspired salad. Cauliflower takes on a wonderful nutty flavour when roasted, and the chunks of pitta add a lovely texture. Reserve a few pomegranate seeds to scatter over at the end to pretty this up a little.

CAULIFLOWER AND TAHINI SALAD

2 small cauliflowers, cut into florets, stalks removed

1 tsp cumin

1 tsp ground coriander

2 garlic cloves, thinly sliced

1 tbsp extra virgin olive oil

Pink Himalayan salt and ground black pepper

¼ bunch coriander, leaves picked and chopped

¼ bunch flat-leaf parsley, leaves picked and chopped

50g toasted pine nuts

2 tbsp currants, soaked in water for 10–15 minutes

Seeds of ½ pomegranate

1 pitta bread, toasted and broken into pieces

FOR THE DRESSING

100g natural yoghurt

65g tahini paste

80ml lemon juice

80ml olive oil

Preheat the oven to 200°C/400°F/gas mark 6. Put the cauliflower florets into a baking dish, sprinkle over the spices, garlic and olive oil, and season with salt and pepper. Toss everything together to make sure the cauliflower is well coated. Roast for 20 minutes, or until tender and lightly golden. Set aside to cool for 10 minutes.

To make the dressing, put all the ingredients in a small bowl and whisk until smooth.

To serve, put the cooled cauliflower in a large bowl and pour over the dressing. Add the herbs, pine nuts, currants, and pomegranate seeds then season to taste. Finally, toss through the toasted pitta bread.

SERVES 4–6

This light salad is a brilliant meal for one, full of vibrant flavours but low carb and low calorie. Alternatively, you could make this as a starter to eat before a Thai curry main. Do make sure you serve immediately, as ingredients will become soggy quite quickly.

GREEN PAPAYA SALAD

1 small green papaya, peeled and very thinly sliced

1 tbsp grated palm sugar

1 garlic clove, grated

1 red bird eye chilli, finely chopped

5 green beans, cut into 2.5 cm lengths

1 tbsp roasted peanuts, coarsely chopped

1 tbsp fish sauce

1 tbsp tamarind water

4 cherry plum tomatoes, halved

Juice of 1 lime

5 cooked medium tiger prawns, peeled, deveined and sliced in half lengthways

In a large mixing bowl, combine the papaya with the palm sugar, garlic, chilli and green beans. Add the peanuts, fish sauce, tamarind water, tomatoes, lime juice and toss well to combine. Transfer to a serving plate, top with the tiger prawns and serve immediately.

SERVES 1–2

This salad is all about a good balance of flavours and textures; crunch and creaminess from pecans, soft, salty sharpness from feta, firm and sweet beetroot and a tangy but aromatic dressing.

ROASTED BEETROOT, PECAN AND FETA SALAD

4–6 baby or small beetroot, peeled, trimmed and quartered

1 tbsp olive oil

2 sprigs thyme

Salt and ground black pepper

2 large handfuls of rocket

100g feta cheese, crumbled

Seeds of 1 pomegranate

30g pecan nuts, toasted

FOR THE DRESSING

¼ tsp dill or fennel seeds

1 tsp peppercorns

2 tbsp chopped dill

1 tbsp white wine vinegar

2 tbsp olive oil

SERVES 4

Preheat the oven to 190°C/380°F/gas mark 5. Put the beetroot in a small roasting tin, then drizzle with oil, add the thyme and season generously with salt and pepper. Roast for around 45 minutes, or until until the beetroot are tender. Remove from the oven and allow to cool.

Meanwhile, prepare the dill dressing. Coarsely crush the fennel seeds and peppercorns in a pestle and mortar, then transfer to bowl and whisk in the other ingredients.

To serve, divide the rocket between four plates, then add the beetroot, followed by the feta, pomegranate seeds and pecans. Finally, drizzle over the dill dressing.

This fabulously simple salad is inspired by childhood memories. The original was made with finely chopped crab, but we like it with good chunks of crayfish for a little more texture, and the same tart, piquant sherry vinegar dressing and the fragrant scent of fresh coriander leaves.

CRAYFISH SALAD

400–600g cooked crayfish, chopped

3–4 ready roasted, marinated peppers, drained and finely chopped

Large handful of coriander leaves, chopped

Rye bread, to serve

FOR THE DRESSING

Juice of 1 lime

300g soured cream

2 red chilli, finely chopped

Salt and ground black pepper

SERVES 4

First, whisk together the dressing ingredients with a generous amount of seasoning.

Put the crayfish meat in a large bowl, then add the peppers and coriander leaves. Drizzle over the dressing and toss gently to combine. Pile the cray fish salad up on four plates, and serve with rye bread.

This smooth, creamy soup has a flavour as intense as its glorious orange colour. Roasting the squash brings out the sweet richness, enhanced with aromatic thyme. We like to serve it with wedges of golden Turkish bread, drizzled with olive oil, then sprinkled with our favourite dukkah.

FRAGRANT BUTTERNUT SQUASH SOUP
IN PUMPKIN BOWLS

4 small pumpkins

3 tbsp olive oil

Salt and ground black pepper

1 butternut squash (about 1kg), peeled, seeded and chopped

2 onions, peeled and chopped

2 sprigs thyme

1.2 litres water

Handful coriander and pumpkin seeds, to serve

Turkish bread, olive oil and dukkah, to serve

SERVES 4

Preheat the oven to 200°C/400°F/gas mark 6. To make the bowls, cut the top off each pumpkin using a paring knife and scoop out the seeds and pulp. Brush the inside walls with oil and sprinkle with salt and pepper. Place the pumpkins and lids on a baking sheet; roast for 30 to 40 minutes, or until the inside flesh is tender.

As the pumpkins roast, put the butternut squash, onions and thyme into a large saucepan. Add 1 litre of the water and bring it to boil, then simmer until the vegetables are just tender. Blend with a hand blender or in a food processor until very smooth, adding the final 200ml water if you need to.

Once the pumpkin bowls are cooked but still holding their shape, ladle the hot soup into them, scatter with seeds then serve with wedges of Turkish bread, olive oil and dukkah.

We like to serve this salad on a large platter as part of a sharing menu; the vibrant colours bring such beauty to a winter table. You'll need a mandolin to slice the beetroot, or a very steady hand when chopping.

BEETROOT SALAD
WITH YUZU DRESSING

1 small golden beetroot, thinly sliced

1 small striped beetroot, thinly sliced

1 Cylindra beetroot or normal beetroot, thinly sliced

1 black radish, thinly sliced

2cm piece of ginger, thinly sliced

1 carrot, thinly sliced

1 tbsp sesame seeds

FOR THE DRESSING

1 tbsp grapeseed oil or light olive oil

2 tbsp soy sauce

1 tbsp yuzu juice

1 tsp finely grated garlic

1 tbsp Japanese mirin

1 tbsp mayonnaise

Arrange the sliced vegetables on a large serving plate or divde between four individual plates.

Whisk together all of the dressing ingredients until smooth, then drizzle over the vegetables. Add a scattering of sesame seeds and serve.

SERVES 4

This punchy salad also works well with chicken, salmon or fried tofu. Once you've tried it, you'll be craving the vibrant flavours on a weekly basis, just like we do!

BEEF AND BASIL SALAD
WITH GLASS NOODLES AND PEANUTS

300g sirloin steak

½ tbsp olive oil

200g glass noodles, cooked, drained and refreshed in cold water

4 spring onions

1 lemongrass stalk, white part only, sliced finely

10 mint leaves

1 small cucumber, thinly sliced

75g roasted peanuts

FOR THE MARINADE

1 tbsp soy sauce

2 tbsp fish sauce

2 tsp sesame oil

FOR THE DRESSING

60ml white vinegar

Juice of 2 limes

2 tbsp fish sauce

3 small red chillies, finely chopped

1 garlic clove, crushed

In a large bowl, combine the steak and all the marinade ingredients. Massage the seasoning into the steak a little then let it marinade for at least 15 minutes, or longer if you have time.

Heat the olive oil in a frying pan and once the pan is very hot, shake off any excess marinade and cook the pieces of steak – 3 to 4 minutes on either side for medium rare. Then allow the meat to rest while you prepare the rest of the salad.

Whisk together the dressing ingredients, then toss with the noodles, spring onions, lemongrass, mint and cucumber in a large bowl. Divide between two plates, then thinly slice the steak and place on top with a drizzle of the meat juices. Scatter with the peanuts and serve immediately.

SERVES 2

We have this salad as a filling lunch on spring days with a chill in the air as well as a relaxed supper in the garden on warm summer evenings. You can try this with apricots and peaches, too, depending on what looks best at the greengrocer.

WARM SMOKED RAINBOW TROUT SALAD
WITH ROSEMARY POTATOES AND NECTARINE

400g kipfler or pink fir apple potatoes, sliced

2 tbsp olive oil

1 lemon, thinly sliced

1 sprig rosemary, needles picked

1 tsp turmeric

4 smoked trout fillets

2 large handfuls of baby cress or frisee

2–3 nectarines, pitted and cut into wedges

8 dill sprigs, finely chopped

Seeds from ½ pomegranate

Salt and ground black pepper

FOR THE DRESSING

2 tbsp olive oil

Zest and juice of 1 lemon

Put the potato slices in a large mixing bowl with the olive oil, lemon, rosemary and turmeric, then toss to combine well. Put a large, heavy-based frying pan over a medium high heat, then add the potatoes and fry until cooked through and golden. Season with salt and pepper then tip out onto a plate.

Preheat the oven to 150°C/300°F/gas mark 3. Using a sharp knife, remove the skin and bones from the smoked trout. Put the fillets onto a baking tray lined with baking paper and bake for 4 minutes, until warmed through.

While the trout warms, mix the dressing ingredients together and use to dress the salad leaves. Divide between four plates, then add the sliced potatoes, followed by the wedges of nectarine and trout. Scatter over the pomegranate seeds, dill and a little extra seasoning, then serve.

SERVES 4

Cashew cream and pomegranate juice really add a vibrancy and interest to this classic combination. If you don't have time to make the cashew cream, or would prefer a little dairy, whisk some ricotta with a little cream until smooth, then add to the plate as you would the cashew cream.

FIG, WALNUT, PROSCIUTTO AND POMEGRANATE SALAD
WITH CASHEW CREAM

1 pomegranate, seeds removed

Large handful of rocket

4 tbsp coarsely chopped walnuts

5 slices of prosciutto

4 large fresh figs, trimmed and cut into eighths

FOR THE CASHEW CREAM

150g unsalted cashew nuts

150ml water

1 tsp cumin

1 tsp sea salt

Ground black pepper

SERVES 4

First, make the cashew cream. Soak the cashew nuts in the water for 1 hour then drain, reserving a couple of tablespoons of the soaking water. Put the nuts and the reserved water into a blender. Add the cumin and seasoning, then blend for 1–2 minutes until smooth and creamy in consistency. If it's too thick to drizzle, add a little extra water.

Next, make the pomegranate dressing. Put the seeds in a sieve over a large bowl, then crush all the seeds to extract as much juice as possible. Throw away the remains and reserve the liquid.

To serve, divide the rocket between four plates, then scatter over the walnuts and slices of prosciutto. Arrange the fig pieces on top, then place a generous spoonful of the cashew cream in the centre and drizzle with the pomegranate juice.

BIG LUNCHES *and* LAZY WEEKENDS

BIG LUNCHES AND LAZY WEEKENDS

Weekends at the café tend to be a more relaxed affair, made all the better with a few indulgent dishes that are just as good to share with a few friends around the table as they are to keep all to yourself.

Our head chef is constantly experimenting with local, seasonal produce, vibrant spices and specialist ingredients, but you can expect dishes such as roasted quail with golden raisins, central European slow-cooked stews and fresh British seafood. This chapter is a collection of some of our favourite recipes that you'll always see on the menu.

This is one of the most simple yet impressive recipes we love to make. Rump is a particularly flavoursome cut and works well when you want something akin to a roasting joint but don't have enough people around the table to demolish it.

GRILLED HERBY LAMB
WITH BABY CHERRY TOMATOES

2 tbsp olive oil

4 rosemary sprigs,
leaves picked

Small bunch of mint,
leaves picked

Salt and ground black pepper

4 lamb rumps, around 250g
each, fat trimmed

350g cherry tomatoes

Small bunch of basil,
leaves picked

2 heads of chicory,
halved lengthways

SERVES 4

To make the marinade, combine the olive oil, rosemary and mint then season with salt and black pepper. Put the lamb in a non-reactive bowl or dish, then pour over the marinade, turning to coat evenly. Cover with cling film and leave to marinate in the fridge for about 8 hours, or preferably overnight.

You can cook the lamb rumps either by grilling from start to finish on a barbecue with a lid, or charring the lamb on the grill and then finishing in the oven. To cook the lamb in a griddle pan and then roast, heat the oven to 220°C/440°F/gas mark 8. Put a griddle pan over a high heat until smoking, then brown the lamb well on all sides and put on a roasting tray. Roast for 30–35 minutes, or until medium rare. Remove from the oven, cover with foil and leave to rest for 15 minutes while you prepare the rest of the dish.

Put a little oil in a frying pan over a medium heat, then add the tomatoes. Cover with a lid or some foil then cook for 5–10 minutes until warm, tender, and starting to lose their shape. Stir through the basil.

Next, heat a griddle pan over a medium heat, brush with a little oil then add the chicory cut-side down. Cook until just charred and season with sea salt.

To serve, slice the lamb across the grain, then put on the plate with the grilled chicory. Dress with the warm tomatoes and serve.

This dish is perfect for sharing with friends; you can serve this on individual plates if you like, but for maximum impact, we put it on two serving platters so every can just dig in. The bitterness of radicchio is a great foil to the punchy dressing.

QUAIL WITH RADICCHIO AND GOLDEN RAISINS

6 quails, spatchcocked

2 garlic gloves, crushed

150ml olive oil

4 sprigs of thyme

Salt and ground black pepper

1 bunch of flat leaf parsley, chopped

1 bunch of chives, chopped

2 shallots, sliced

1 head of radicchio, leaves separated

2 tbsp chopped hazelnuts

FOR THE GOLDEN RAISIN PURÉE

115g golden raisins

Sea salt

FOR THE DRESSING

2 tbsp sherry vinegar

25g Dijon mustard

80ml olive oil

Salt and ground black pepper

SERVES 6

First, prepare the quails. You can ask your butcher to spatchcock the birds for you, or, to do this yourself. Then put the birds in a large, non-reactive metal or glass bowl, mix with the garlic, oil and thyme, then season well. Allow to marinade for at least 30 minutes.

Next, make the golden raisin purée. Put the raisins in a small saucepan and cover with water. Bring to the boil, then immediately take off the heat and strain. Put the raisins in a blender and blend to a purée, adding a little water if it needs loosening. Add a pinch of salt to taste.

Make the dressing by whisking the vinegar and mustard in a small bowl, then slowly drizzle in the oil, continuing to whisk until emulsified, and season. Mix the herbs with the shallots and dressing to taste. Adjust the seasoning if necessary.

To cook the quails, preheat the oven to 180°C/350°F/gas mark 6, then heat a large, heavy-based frying pan over a high heat and cook the birds for 2–3 minutes skin-side down until golden brown; you may need to do this in batches. Put the birds on a couple of baking sheets, skin-side up, then roast in the oven for 10–12 minutes, until cooked through. Rest for 2–3 minutes while you assemble the dish.

Divide the raisin purée between two serving plates. Dress the radicchio with the herb and shallot mix, then arrange on the plates. Place the cooked quails on top, then sprinkle over the chopped hazelnuts and serve immediately.

This meat-free dish is one of our most popular lunch dishes; the crunch of the seed-coated fried tofu and the distinctive flavour of shiitake will keep your palate guessing from one mouthful to the next.

SESAME TOFU
WITH SHIITAKE MUSHROOMS

FOR THE AGEDASHI SAUCE

20g dried shiitake mushrooms

400ml boiling water

1 tsp grated fresh ginger

2 tbsp soy sauce, plus a little extra for the mushrooms

1 tbsp mirin

1 tsp sesame oil, plus extra for frying

2 tbsp cornflour

1 tbsp sesame seeds

1 tbsp nigella seeds

300g silken tofu, cut into 3cm cubes

3 tbsp extra virgin oil

1 spring onion, finely sliced

Handful of basil

2 radishes, very thinly sliced

Cress leaves, to serve (optional)

SERVES 2

Soak the mushrooms in the boiling water until soft; around 15 minutes. Remove from the liquid and squeeze dry, then strain the liquid into a small pot and add the ginger, soy, mirin and sesame oil. Bring to a gentle simmer and let it reduce by half – this will take about 12 minutes.

While the mushroom liquid is reducing, heat a drizzle of sesame oil in a frying pan over a medium high heat. Fry the mushrooms, with a dash of soy sauce, until golden brown.

Next, prepare the tofu. Combine the cornflour, sesame and nigella seeds, then season well with salt and pepper. Add the tofu and gently coat with sesame cornflour mix.

Heat the oil in a large frying pan over a medium-high heat. Lightly fry the tofu on all sides until golden and crisp. Divide the tofu between bowls, scatter over the mushrooms and spoon over the agedashi sauce. Garnish with spring onion, radish and cress leaves.

Gently cooked quince adds a bold, tart edge to this game roast, packed with aromatic winter herbs. Serve with with buttered couscous, creamy mashed potatoes or even herb-flecked rice.

ROAST GUINEA FOWL WITH QUINCE

1 tbsp dried thyme

1 tbsp dried oregano

5 tbsp olive oil

Sea salt and ground black pepper

1 bunch fresh oregano

1 guinea fowl, around 1.2kg

1 green apple, cut into wedges

3 quince, peeled and cut into thin wedges

SERVES 4

Preheat the oven to 180°C/350°F/gas mark 4. Whisk together 4 tablespoons of the olive oil with the thyme, dried oregano, salt and pepper then rub over the guinea fowl, inside and out. Put the apple wedges and fresh oregano into the cavity of the bird and tie the legs with kitchen string to secure. Place in a deep roasting tray, then pour 300ml water around the bird and cover loosely with foil. Roast for 2 hours, removing the foil for the final 30 minutes to crisp the skin.

Put the quince wedges into a saucepan with 50ml water, cover with a lid then cook over a low heat for 15 minutes, or until just tender. Drain any excess water from the quince, then heat the final tablespoon of olive in a frying pan and cook the quince for 5 minutes, until they start to brown slightly.

To serve, put the guinea fowl on a large platter and place the quince around it.

There's nothing more satisfying than catching courgette flowers before they wilt, but if you haven't grown your own, you'll be able to find them online or at any good greengrocers. Feel free to experiment a little; we also like to swap the parmesan for crab meat and the mint for coriander.

STUFFED COURGETTE FLOWERS

Small handful of mint leaves, finely chopped

200g ricotta

2 tbsp finely grated parmesan

18 baby courgettes with flowers attached

Pinch of salt and ground black pepper

1 litre vegetable or light olive oil, for frying

FOR THE BATTER

80g flour

60g cornflour

180ml cold soda water

SERVES 6

Mix together the mint, ricotta and parmesan in a bowl with a generous amount of seasoning.

With your fingers, very carefully pull out the inside stamen of each courgette flower, taking extra care not to rip the outside. Using a teaspoon, carefully push the cheese mixture into the flower, then twist petal ends to enclose and place in a baking dish. Repeat with the rest of the flowers.

Heat a deep-fat fryer or saucepan with the oil to 180°C/350°F or until a small piece of bread sizzles and turns golden in 30 seconds.

Working quickly, mix together the flour and cornflour in a large bowl, then add the soda water and whisk to a smooth batter. Dip flowers in the batter, shake of any of the excess, then fry for 2–4 minutes, until golden. Drain on paper towels, sprinkle with a little salt then serve immediately.

Buying a whole crab is more than worth it for this, and will certainly look pretty spectacular when you put it on the table with a heaped bowl of steamed rice. The same sauce is also fantastic with fried tofu.

BLACK PEPPER CRAB WITH GINGER

1.5kg whole live brown crabs (do not buy dead, uncooked crabs)

2 tbsp vegetable oil

3 garlic cloves

2 banana shallots, sliced

2 red chillies, sliced

25g peeled ginger, in strips

2 tsp fish sauce

1 tbsp dark soy sauce

2 tbsp oyster sauce

2 spring onions, sliced

1 tbsp black peppercorns

1 tbsp Chinese fermented salted black beans, rinsed and chopped

Roughly chopped coriander, to serve

SERVES 4

First, prepare the crab meat. Freeze the crabs for 1 hour beforehand. Bring a large pan of salted water to the boil, then fully submerge the crabs in the water and boil for 15-18 minutes. If necessary, cook individually but allow the water to return to the boil between each one. Leave to cool.

Break off the tail flaps and discard, then break off the claws, cut the body of each crab in half with the legs attached and cut each section into 2 or 3 pieces. Cut the legs in half at the joints with a cleaver. Using the back of a cleaver or knife, carefully crack the claws to remove the meat.

Heat a wok over a high heat. Add the oil and stir fry the crab pieces for 3 minutes. Remove from the wok and drain on paper towels.

Return the wok to a medium-high heat, then add the garlic, shallots, ginger, chillies and cook for a few seconds. Lower the heat to medium and add the fish sauce and 2–3 tablespoons of water. Stir in the soy sauce, oyster sauce and spring onions, then add the peppercorns and beans and cook for another 2 minutes, stirring once or twice. Return the crab pieces to the wok, simmer for 5–7 minutes until the crab has warmed through and liquid has thickened. Scatter with coriander and serve.

Healthy but hearty, simply baked salmon with a spoonful of lemony sweet potato hummus is always a favourite at our lunch service. If you can't find black sesame seeds, white will work well too, as will a traditional hazelnut dukkah.

SALMON FILLETS
WITH SWEET POTATO HUMMUS

4 salmon fillets, skin on

Sea salt and ground black pepper

2 tbsp extra-virgin olive oil

small bunch of watercress

Large handful of mint leaves, roughly torn

Juice of ½ a lemon

2 tsp pistachio dukkah

Black sesame seeds, to serve

Lemon or lime wedges, to serve

FOR THE SWEET POTATO HUMMUS

500g sweet potatoes, peeled and roughly chopped

400g tin chickpeas, rinsed and drained

4 tbsp lemon juice

3 tbsp olive oil

Salt and ground black pepper

First, make the sweet potato hummus. Fill a large saucepan with boiling water, add the potatoes and reduce to a simmer, then cover and cook for around 15–20 minutes, until tender. Drain the potatoes and allow to cool a little before transferring to a food processor. Add the chickpeas, lemon juice and oil then blend until smooth. Season with salt and pepper and allow to cool completely.

Preheat the oven to 180°C/350°F/gas mark 4. Brush the salmon with 1 tablespoon of the olive oil and season generously. Bake for 5–10 minutes or until the salmon is golden and just cooked through.

Place the remaining oil, watercress, mint, lemon juice and a little seasoning in a large bowl then toss together. Divide between the plates, then top with a couple of spoonfuls of sweet potato hummus, the salmon, pistachio dukkah, black sesame seeds and lemon or lime wedges.

SERVES 4

This herby omelette is a great buffet or large lunch party dish;
good value, vegetarian and best made in advance. At the café,
we serve this with some crusty bread and a green salad.

HERB CAKE

9 eggs, beaten

Juice of 1 lemon

1 bunch flat-leaf parsley,
finely chopped

1 leek, finely chopped,
including most of
the green part

1 bunch dill, chopped

1 bunch mint, chopped

2 bunches of chives, chopped

Salt and ground black pepper

100g walnuts, chopped

2 tbsp olive oil

1 tbsp ground sumac

SERVES 6

In a large mixing bowl, whisk together the eggs, lemon juice
and herbs. Season with salt and pepper, then add the chopped
walnuts.

Heat the oil in a 20cm non-stick lidded frying pan, then pour in
the egg mixture and cover with the lid.

After 5 minutes, when the bottom has set, remove the lid,
shaking the frying pan from side to side so a little of the
uncooked mixture runs down the sides. Cover and reduce the
heat, then cook for a further 15 minutes, or until the egg is set.
Then cover the frying pan with a flat plate, flip the pan over
and slide the omlette back into the pan to cook for another 5
minutes.

Once done, slide out onto a plate and sprinkle with sumac.
This can be served warm or cold.

The bold flavours of this one-pot dish belie its simplicity; serve with a simple watercress salad, as suggested, or with some steamed vegetables if you want to make it a little heartier. Once cooked, this will keep well in the freezer for a couple of months.

CHICKEN ## WITH CHESTNUTS AND REDCURRANTS

30ml olive oil

2 onions, thinly sliced

60ml extra virgin olive oil

1kg chicken, cut into 8 pieces

Sea salt and ground black black pepper

1 sprig of rosemary, needles picked and chopped

150g redcurrants

100g cooked chestnuts

100g watercress, to serve

SERVES 4

Heat the olive oil in a large saucepan over medium heat. Add the onion and sweat for 10–15 minutes until golden brown. Then remove from the pan and set aside.

Put the pan back over a high heat with the extra virgin olive oil. Rub the chicken with salt, pepper and rosemary and fry the pieces for around 3–4 minutes, until golden. Then return the onions to the pan and add the redcurrants and chestnuts.

Cover and cook for 30 minutes, until the chicken is tender. Serve immediately with watercress sprigs.

Skirt steaks are much better value than other cuts but require very careful cooking; a minute over and you'll end up with something a lot chewier than you intended.

Rest time is crucial here, so you can spend those 5 minutes focussing on getting the rest of the meal on the table.

SKIRT STEAKS
WITH CHIMICHURRI SAUCE AND SALSA

1 tbsp olive oil

400g pieces of skirt steak,
at room temperature

salt and ground black pepper

FOR THE CHIMICHURRI SAUCE

250ml olive oil

100ml white wine vinegar

Large bunch of coriander,
finely chopped

3 garlic cloves, coarsely chopped

1 tbsp dried chilli flakes

FOR THE SALSA

125ml olive oil

50ml white wine vinegar

3 ripe Roma tomatoes,
seeds removed, finely diced

2 red peppers,
seeds removed, finely diced

1 onion, finely diced

2 long green chillies, thinly sliced

To make the chimichurri sauce, whisk together all the ingredients in a bowl and set aside. Next, mix together all the salsa ingredients and set aside.

Rub the olive oil into the skirt steak and season. Preheat a chargrill pan over medium-high heat. Chargrill the meat, turning occasionally until cooked to your liking (3–4 minutes for medium-rare).

Set aside to rest for a few minutes then serve alongside the salsa and chimichurri sauce.

SERVES 4

This vibrant rice dish will become a household classic, the combination of sweet but sharp dried fruit, aromatic herbs and buttery rice working well with all manner of grilled meats and even fish.

WILD RICE
WITH CRANBERRIES

250g mix of brown and wild rice

500ml water

100g peas

100g dried cranberries

100g raisins

30g dried apricots, chopped

100g ready cooked chestnuts, roughly chopped

1 tbsp dried dill

1 tbsp dried oregano

1 tbsp dried thyme

Salt and ground black pepper

150g unsalted butter

1 tbsp turmeric

12 Bavarian or herby sausages, cooked to serve (optional)

Put the rice in a large saucepan with the water then bring to a simmer and cook for 30 minutes. At this point, add the peas, fruit and chestnuts, dried herbs and seasoning, stir to combine, then add the butter and turmeric, but do not stir, leave to sit on top of the rice.

Cover and cook for another 15 minutes, until all the liquid has absorbed, then serve with or without the sausages.

SERVES 2–3

Don't be fooled by the limited ingredients, this stew packs in some bold flavours. The dried sour plums may take some tracking down, but it is more than worth it for the tart tang of them to balance the rich beef.

BEEF STEW
WITH MINT AND SOUR PLUMS

1 onion, chopped

500g stewing steak, chopped

3 tbsp canned chickpeas

4 dried sour plums, chopped

1 large potato, chopped

1 tomato, chopped

Salt and ground black pepper

Small handful of mint leaves, chopped

SERVES 2

Preheat the oven to 190°C/375F/gas mark 6, then divide the onions, beef, chickpeas and sour plums between two single-serving casserole dishes, or one larger one. Pour 500ml of water into each, cover and cook for 30 minutes.

After this time is up, add the potato and tomato with plenty of seasoning and cook for another 40 minutes. Once the meat is tender and the gravy has thickened, sprinkle over the chopped mint and serve.

Make a vegetarian version of this hearty lunch by swapping out the beef mince for a couple of finely diced red or yellow peppers. At Brown and Rosie's, we use beef tomatoes, but if you can't get hold of any then simply stuff the filling into several smaller tomatoes and reduce the final cooking time a little.

STUFFED BAKED TOMATOES

8 large tomatoes

2 tbsp olive oil

1½ onions, finely chopped

500g lean beef mince

1 small bunch of fresh oregano finely chopped

½ small bunch of coriander finely chopped

Handful of basil leaves, chopped

1 tsp dried dill

1 tsp dried rosemary

1 tbsp turmeric

salt and pepper to taste

400g tin chopped tomatoes

SERVES 4

Preheat oven to 200°C/400°F/gas mark 6. Slice the top off each tomato and scoop out the inside with a teaspoon, keeping the tomato lid intact and reserving the scooped flesh.

Heat the oil over a medium heat, then add the onion, beef, herbs, turmeric and chopped tomatoes together with the scooped inside of the fresh tomatoes. Reduce the heat and cover, then cook for about 15 minutes, stirring from time to time, until the beef is cooked and the sauce has thickened.

Allow the filling to cool a little, then spoon into the tomatoes, drizzle over a little olive oil and bake for 20 minutes, until the tomatoes have softened but still hold their shape.

Cooking octopus is far less intimidating than it sounds, and is guaranteed to impress. If you want to serve this as part of a small plates meal, then serve without the spaghetti.

OCTOPUS WITH SPAGHETTI AND ROMESCO SAUCE

2 celery stalks, roughly chopped

1 onion, roughly chopped

700g Roma tomatoes, roughly chopped

½ tsp coriander seeds

½ tsp peppercorns

1 bay leaf

1 leek, roughly chopped

2 sprigs each of dill, basil, thyme

200ml red wine

400g baby octopus

2 tbsp olive oil

250g wholewheat spaghetti

FOR THE ROMESCO SAUCE

3 whole red peppers

2 shallots, roughly chopped

2 tbsp almonds, roughly chopped

2 tbsp sherry vinegar

2 tbsp olive oil

Salt and ground black pepper

2 tsp smoked paprika

Juice of 1 lemon

Place the celery, onions, tomatoes, coriander seeds, peppercorns, bay leaf, leek, herbs, wine and octopus in a large saucepan. Cover with water, then bring to a simmer and cook gently for 90 minutes.

Meanwhile, make the romesco sauce. Roast the red peppers over an open flame; once blackened, put into a bowl and cover over with cling film to let them steam. Once the peppers have cooled a little, remove the skin and seeds, then roughly chop. Put them in a blender with the shallots, almonds and a little bit of vinegar, then blend until smooth. Reduce the speed of the blender then drizzle in the olive oil and add a little water if it is too thick. Season with salt, pepper, smoked paprika, lemon juice and the rest of the vinegar.

Cook the spaghetti according to packet instructions. When ready to serve, heat the olive oil in a frying pan, add the cooked octopus and fry for around 10 seconds on each side, until lightly browned.

Toss the romesco sauce with the spaghetti, divide between four bowls then top with the octopus.

SERVES 4

Cuttlefish is a fantastic and better value alternative to squid; try adding some finely diced chorizo for a touch of smokiness.

CUTTLEFISH WITH RICE AND TOMATOES

6 small cuttlefish, bones and ink sack removed and cleaned

300ml red wine

250g mixed brown and wild rice

3 large tomatoes, finely chopped

1 yellow pepper, finely chopped

1 courgette, finely chopped

1 small red onion, finely chopped

1 tbsp dried dill

1 tbsp dried oregano

1 small bunch of fresh coriander, chopped

Salt and ground black pepper

1 tbsp olive oil

Put the cuttlefish and red wine into a large lidded frying pan over a medium heat. Cover and cook until the cuttlefish is soft. Drain off some excess wine and leave the cuttlefish in the pan.

As the cuttlefish cooks, cook the rice following packet instructions. Once cooked, mix with the vegetables, herbs and seasoning.

Stuff the cuttlefish with the mixture and close by piercing each side with a toothpick. Heat the olive oil in the frying pan, then cook the cuttlefish over a medium heat for 15 minutes. You can serve as a cold or warm starter on its own.

SERVES 6

This dish is an explosion of flavour; served with steamed rice, or even flatbreads, as an alternative to a BBQ in summer.

SLOW ROASTED PORK WITH PINEAPPLE
ON BANANA LEAVES

1 pineapple, peeled, cored and chopped into 4cm chunks

1.5kg pork shoulder

500g banana leaves (available fresh or frozen at Asian supermarkets)

FOR THE MARINADE

2 tbsp olive oil, plus extra for rubbing

1 tsp chilli flakes

2 tsp dried oregano

Juice and zest of 1 orange

1 tsp sea salt flakes

FOR THE AVOCADO YOGHURT

2 avocados, stone removed, flesh chopped

100ml Greek yoghurt

Juice of 1 lime

1 chilli, finely chopped to taste

1 tbsp finely chopped chives

FOR THE POMEGRANATE ONIONS

1 red onion, halved and thinly slices

1 tsp sumac

2 tbsp pomegranate juice

First, make the marinade. Put all of the ingredients into a food processor and blend until smooth.

Place the pork in a large non-reactive bowl, then pour over the marinade, rubbing in to make sure the meat is well coated. Cover and chill for 3 hours, or preferably overnight.

Preheat the oven to 180°C/350°F/gas mark 6. Place the pineapple chunks on a baking tray to roast for 40 minutes, then set aside.

Turn the oven up to 250°C/500°F/gas mark 9. Line an ovenproof dish with the banana leaves so that they are overlapping. Place the pork into the dish and pour all the marinade from the bowl over the top. Fold the leaves over to encase the pork. Cover the dish tightly with foil and bake for 3 hours.

For the avocado yoghurt, combine all the ingredients in a bowl and blend with a hand blender to a smooth purée. Season with salt and stir through the chives then set aside.

Next, make the pomegranate onions. Bring the pomegranate juice to the boil, then pour into a medium bowl, add the onion and sumac and chill until needed.

Once cooked, remove the pork from the dish, reserving all the juices. Shred the meat into chunky pieces using two forks then pour over the juices, making sure to coat the meat evenly. Transfer the pork to a serving dish, scatter with the roasted pineapple and the pomegranate onions. Serve with the avocado yoghurt.

SERVES 4

Duck legs are much better value than their rich, fatty meat suggests; served with a vibrant salad, it's one of the easiest dinner party mains with wow-factor we can think of.

DUCK WITH QUINOA AND POMEGRANATE

4 duck legs

Juice and zest of 1 orange

1 tbsp juniper berries, lightly crushed

1 garlic clove, crushed

3 bay leaves

8 sprigs thyme

½ tsp turmeric

1 tsp sea salt

Ground black pepper

FOR THE SALAD

400g quinoa

750ml water

1 bunch of cavolo nero, finely shredded

1 bunch of watercress

1 tbsp almonds

100g raisins

Seeds from ½ pomegranate

FOR THE TRUFFLE DRESSING

1 tbsp Dijon mustard

2 tbsp lemon juice

2 tbsp truffle oil

Place the duck legs in a non-reactive dish to fit snuggly in a single layer. In a small bowl, combine the orange juice and zest, juniper berries, garlic, bay leaves, thyme, turmeric, salt and a little black pepper. Pour this over the duck, turning the legs until evenly coated. Cover with cling film and allow to marinate in the fridge for at least 12 hours, or for best results 24 hours.

Preheat oven to 180°C/350°F/gas mark 4, then place duck legs in a baking dish, in a single layer. Lightly prick the skin of each duck leg then cook for around 90 minutes, until the meat is very tender and the skin is crisp. Leave in the dish to cool completely.

As the duck cooks, make the salad. Put the quinoa in a saucepan with 750ml water and simmer for 15–20 minutes. Allow to cool, then tip into a large bowl and mix with the cavolo nero, watercress, almonds and raisins. Whisk together the ingredients for the dressing, then toss with the salad.

To serve, spread the salad out onto a serving plate, top with the duck legs and sprinkle over the pomegranate seeds.

SERVES 4

The sweetness of peaches and aromatic thyme is a classic combination for pork, for very good reason. This is perhaps our favourite summer Sunday roast; best served with crusty bread for mopping up the juices.

ROAST PORK
WITH FRESH PEACHES AND THYME

2 tbsp wholegrain mustard

1 tbsp coarse sea salt flakes

3 sprigs of rosemary, needles picked

2 tbsp thyme leaves

Ground black pepper

2kg boneless centre cut pork loin, skin on, rolled and tied with string

6 small peaches, stones removed and halved

1 tbsp balsamic vinegar

1½ tbsp olive oil

SERVES 4

Preheat oven to 230°C/440°F/gas mark 8. Mix the mustard, salt flakes, rosemary, 1 tablespoon of the thyme leaves and some black pepper in a small bowl.

Drizzle the pork with 1 tablespoon of the oil then rub the mustard and salt mixture over the skin and into the cuts. Put the pork into a roasting tin and cook for 35 minutes, or until the rind crackles.

Reduce the oven temperature to 180°C/350°F/gas mark 4. Add the peaches to the roasting tin and roast for 1 hour, or until the peaches are tender and the juices run clear when a skewer is inserted into the centre of the pork. Transfer the pork to a large plate and cover loosely with foil. Spoon off as much fat as you can from the juices in the roasting tin.

To serve, carve the pork into thick slices, then place on a platter with the peaches and some seasoning before drizzling with the balsamic vinegar and olive oil.

This is a knock-out Sunday lunch for warmer months, though the cannellini bean spread is also delicious on toasted sourdough, topped with roasted tomatoes.

ROAST BEEF RIB
WITH HERBY CANNELLINI BEAN SPREAD

½ bunch thyme leaves

3 garlic cloves, crushed

1 tbsp olive oil

Salt and ground black pepper

2kg rib of beef

FOR CANNELLINI BEAN SPREAD

2 x 400g tins cannellini beans, drained

3 tbsp tahini paste

2 garlic cloves, crushed

2–3 tbsp extra virgin olive oil

2 tbsp lemon juice

Small bunch of flat leaf parsley, leaves picked

Small bunch of basil or coriander, leaves picked

½ small bunch of mint, leaves picked

FOR THE BEANS

300g green beans, topped

1 tbsp olive oil

1 garlic clove, finely chopped

115g pistachio kernels, roughly chopped

Salt and ground black pepper

Small bunch of flat leaf parsley, leaves chopped

Preheat the oven to 200°C/400°F/gas mark 6. Combine the thyme leaves, garlic and half the olive oil in a small bowl, rub over the beef and season to taste. Place in a large roasting tin, roast for 15 minutes, then reduce to 180°C/350°F/gas mark 4 and cook until medium rare, 1–1¼ hours, turning halfway through. Transfer to a plate, reserving the pan juices, then cover with foil and rest while you make the accompaniments.

To make the spread, put all ingredients in a food processor and blend, adding a little more salt and pepper if needed.

Cook the green beans in a saucepan of boiling water for 2–3 minutes, or until the beans are bright green with a little bite, then drain and refresh in cold water. Heat the oil in a frying pan, add the garlic and cook for 1 minute until fragrant then add the beans and pistachios to the pan. Cook, tossing for 2 minutes or until the beans are heated through. Season with salt and pepper and stir in the parsley.

Slice the rib of beef, then serve with the green beans and a little spread.

SERVES 6

Stuffing fish with dried fruit and nuts is a much more interesting alternative to the usual aromatics. Hazelnuts work well with most fish, but you'll need something with the firm texture of snapper to stand up to walnuts. As a quick meal for one, try stirring the stuffing ingredients through couscous (minus the onion and garlic) and serving with a pan-fried fillet of white fish.

SNAPPER
WITH WALNUT, HAZELNUT AND RAISIN STUFFING ON BANANA LEAVES

1.8–2kg whole snapper, cleaned and scaled

2 tbsp olive oil

Salt and ground black pepper

½ bunch of fresh mint, leaves picked, plus extra to serve

2 shallots, roughly chopped

1 banana leaf, fresh coriander leaves and lemon slices, to serve

FOR THE STUFFING

200g mix of walnuts and hazelnuts

1 onion, roughly chopped

1 garlic clove, chopped

150g raisins

3 tbsp pomegranate molasses

1 tbsp olive oil

Salt and ground black pepper

First, make the stuffing. Put the nuts, onions and garlic into a food processor and blend until smooth. Transfer this into a bowl and add the raisins, pomegranate molasses and olive oil. Mix well, season to taste and set aside.

Rinse the snapper inside and out, then pat dry with paper towels. Rub the skin of the fish with olive oil and seasoning. Fill the cavity with the stuffing.

Preheat the oven to 190°C/375F/gas mark 4. Put the fish in a deep roasting tin, scatter over the mint leaves and shallots, cover with foil, then roast until cooked through, around 35–40 minutes.

To serve, lay the banana leaf over a large serving plate. Once the fish is cooked, carefully lift it from the tray and place on top of the leaf. Pour over some of the cooking juices and add slices of lemon and some fresh coriander leaves.

SERVES 4

This recipe is the epitome of a simple crowd pleaser;
the spices bring the lamb to life and the carrots add a little
crunch and sweetness – perfect for a family gathering.

SLOW-ROASTED LEG OF LAMB
WITH RAINBOW CARROTS AND HERB YOGHURT

2.5kg leg of lamb

1 tsp ground sumac

¼ tsp ground coriander

½ tsp sea salt

1 tbsp olive oil

2 bunches rainbow carrots, peeled and trimmed, larger carrots halved lengthwise

FOR THE LAMB MARINADE

2 garlic cloves

2 tbsp finely chopped oregano leaves

3 tbsp olive oil

2 tbsp sea salt

FOR THE HERB YOGHURT

200g Greek yoghurt

1 tbsp roughly chopped coriander

Salt and ground black pepper

First, make the marinade. Whisk the garlic, oregano, olive oil and salt together in a small bowl, then place the lamb leg in a deep baking tray and rub the marinade all over the meat. Cover with foil and let it marinate in the fridge for a few hours, or overnight.

Preheat the oven 150°C/300°F/gas mark 3. Uncover the marinated lamb, then recover the whole tray tightly with foil and cook for 4½–5 hours, removing the foil for the last hour of roasting to crisp up the skin.

In the last 45 minutes of the lamb's cooking time, prepare the carrots. Combine the sumac, coriander and salt in a small bowl. Toss the carrots and olive oil together in a large baking tray, then sprinkle over the sumac and coriander mixture, continuing to toss until the spices are evenly distributed. Place the tray in the oven with the lamb and roast for 30-40 minutes, until the carrots are just tender.

Next, make the herb yoghurt by whisking together the yoghurt and coriander with a generous amount of seasoning. Chill until ready to serve.

Once the lamb is cooked, transfer it onto a serving plate and pour the juices from the tray into a small jug, skimming off most of the fat. Place the carrots in a serving dish with an extra sprinkling of sea salt. Serve immediately with the herb yoghurt.

SERVES 8

LUNCH ON THE GO

Whether you're rushing between meetings or trying to make the most of a flying visit to the capital, nutrition and flavour can often take a back seat at lunchtime as people opt for convenience. But here at Brown and Rosie's, our lunch menu is full of quick, wholesome and delicious ideas to keep you going.

From pulled pork with cabbage slaw to steak with red pepper relish, we've got some great ideas for sandwiches, wraps and rolls. Our aubergine stacks and pumpkin and goat's cheese savoury strudel would make great starter options too.

A steak sandwich is the king of crowd pleasers. This punchy tomato and pepper relish will keep well in the fridge for a couple of days, so any leftovers can be used with a simple toasted cheese sandwich or even a grilled salmon fillet.

STEAK SANDWICH
WITH RED PEPPER RELISH

4 fillet steaks, around 150g each and 2.5cm thick

2 tbsp olive oil

¼ small white cabbage, very thinly sliced

¼ small red cabbage, very thinly sliced

8 slices of rye sourdough bread

Small handful coriander leaves, to serve

4 basil leaves, to serve

FOR THE DRESSING

3 tbsp olive oil

1 tbsp white vinegar

Juice of ½ lemon

Salt and ground black pepper

FOR THE RED PEPPER RELISH

½ tbsp olive oil

1 red onion, finely chopped

2 red peppers, finely chopped

3 tomatoes, finely chopped

1 chilli, deseeded and finely chopped

Sea salt

Pinch of cayenne pepper

Small handful of basil leaves, shredded

First, make the relish. Heat the olive oil in a frying pan over a medium heat, then cook the onion for a couple of minutes, until it begins to soften. Add the peppers, tomatoes and chilli with a little sea salt and cayenne, cooking for another 5–10 minutes, until the tomato has broken down and thickened a little. Allow to cool, then add the shredded basil. Check the seasoning, then set aside.

Next, whisk together the dressing ingredients, until emulsified, then toss together with the white and red cabbage.

Generously season the steak on both sides. Add the olive oil to a griddle or frying pan over a very high heat, then cook the steaks for about 4–5 minutes on each side for medium to well done, or more or less time depending on how you like it. Remove the steaks from the pan and allow to rest for 5 minutes then slice thickly on the diagonal.

While the steaks rest, toast the bread. To assemble the sandwich, spread some relish on half of the toast slices, top each with basil and coriander leaves, slices of steak and some cabbage. Sandwich together with the other slices of bread and serve immediately.

SERVES 4

It feels as though the world has gone mad for pulled pork, and we like to think our version is one of the best. This recipe makes a lot pork, so any leftovers can go in the fridge for the next day.

PULLED PORK SLIDERS
WITH A LIGHT CABBAGE-SLAW

2kg boned pork shoulder

3 tbsp paprika

1 tbsp mustard

Sea salt and ground black pepper

Olive oil, for drizzling

100ml water

Fresh mint leaves, to serve

Bread rolls, to serve

FOR THE SAUCE

3 tbsp cider vinegar

120ml mild American-style mustard

1 tbsp tomato purée

1 garlic clove

75g brown sugar

Salt and ground black pepper

FOR THE CABBAGE SLAW

200ml soured cream

Juice of ½ a lemon

1 tbsp redcurrant jelly

Sea salt and ground black pepper

½ red cabbage, very thinly sliced

¼ red onion, peeled and finely shredded

Slash the skin of the pork about 1cm deep, then rub all over with the paprika, mustard, salt, plenty of ground black pepper and a good splash of olive oil. Cover and let marinate in the fridge or at least a couple of hours, or preferably overnight.

Preheat the oven to 190°C/380°F/gas mark 6. Place the pork in a roasting tin and add 100ml water. Loosely wrap in foil, then cook for around 4 hours, basting every 45 minutes, until the meat is meltingly tender.

When the meat has around 30 minutes cooking time left, make the dressing for the cabbage slaw. Combine the soured cream, lemon juice and redcurrant jelly in a bowl, and season with salt and pepper to taste. Put the cabbage and red onion in a bowl, then toss with the dressing and another pinch of salt and ground black pepper.

About 15 minutes before the end of cooking time, make the sauce. Combine the vinegar, mustard, tomato purée, garlic, sugar, salt, and black pepper in a saucepan over medium heat and simmer gently for 10 minutes.

When the pork is ready, pull apart with two forks, roughly shredding the meat, then pile up on a dish. Pour over about 4 tablespoons of the sauce, scatter over some fresh mint, then toss together. Serve with the cabbage slaw and bread rolls for people to assemble themselves.

SERVES 4

We love this wholesome, healthy sandwich; the crunch of the red cabbage and creamy avocado provide good contrasting texture. If you're taking this in your lunchbox, wrap it tightly in foil so you don't lose any of the filling.

THE ULTIMATE SALAD SANDWICH

2 carrots, peeled and sliced into fine strips

¼ red cabbage, very thinly sliced

1 teaspoon of olive oil

1 teaspoon of vinegar

Salt and ground black pepper

8 thick slices of sourdough bread

1 avocado, peeled, stoned and sliced

2 tomatoes, thinly sliced

Handful of coriander, leaves picked

SERVES 4

Put the carrots and red cabbage in a bowl, pour over the olive oil and vinegar and add a generous amount of seasoning, then toss to combine.

To assemble, top four slices of bread with the avocado and tomato slices, followed by the carrot and red cabbage mix. Scatter over some coriander leaves, then top with the remaining sourdough slices.

If pumpkin is out of season, try using butternut squash or even aubergine in this strudel. Perfect for a make ahead lunch, we've also made them as individual parcels for a vegetarian option at Christmas, swapping the basil for a handful of dried cranberries.

PUMPKIN & GOAT'S CHEESE SAVOURY STRUDEL

1kg pumpkin, cut into 2cm cubes

1 tsp cumin seeds

Extra virgin olive oil

1 fennel bulb, thinly sliced

200g soft goat's cheese

½ tsp finely chopped basil

Ground black pepper

5 sheets filo pastry

1 tsp sesame seeds

Watercress salad, to serve

SERVES 4

Preheat the oven to 200°C/400°F/gas mark 6. Put the pumpkin in a roasting tin, sprinkle over the cumin and drizzle with 2 tablespoons of oil. Toss to coat well then roast for about 25 minutes, until tender. Set aside to cool slightly.

Meanwhile, drizzle a little oil into a large, non-stick frying pan and cook the fennel for 5 minutes, or until softened. Put the fennel and pumpkin in a bowl, add the goat's cheese, basil and a good grinding of black pepper, then gently stir to combine.

On a flat work surface, brush a sheet of filo pastry with olive oil, lay another sheet on top and brush again. Repeat the process with the remaining pastry to make a laminated stack of 5 layers. Spoon the filling mixture along one long side of the pastry, leaving a 3cm border. Fold in the short ends then roll up to create a long log, enclosing all the filling.

Transfer the strudel to a baking tray, brush with oil and sprinkle over the seasame seeds. Bake for 20–25 minutes, until crisp and golden. Leave to cool for a few minutes before slicing and serve with a watercress salad.

Chicken, avocado and mango is a classic, summer combination; the turmeric marinade adds a little savoury depth to the meat. This works equally well in a toasted ciabatta roll, or even wrapped up in a warm naan bread.

CHICKEN SANDWICH
WITH MANGO AND AVOCADO

2 skinless chicken breasts

1 tbsp turmeric

Olive oil

Salt and ground black pepper

8 slices seeded bread, toasted

1 avocado, peeled, stone removed and mashed

Large handful of frisee lettuce

2 tomatoes, thinly sliced

1 cucumber, thinly sliced

FOR THE MANGO SALSA

½ mango, peeled and diced

1 shallot, finely chopped

Juice and zest of 1 lime

Small handful of coriander leaves, roughly chopped

SERVES 4

Place the chicken breasts on a chopping board, then carefully, with a sharp knife, slice through the middle of each lengthways, making four thin pieces. Lay the pieces flat in a dish. Whisk the turmeric into the olive oil with some seasoning and pour over the chicken, turning them to coat evenly. Marinate in the fridge for 30 minutes.

Next, make the mango salsa by putting all the ingredients in a bowl with a little salt and mixing well.

Heat 1 tablespoon olive oil in a frying pan over a medium heat, then remove the chicken from the marinade, shaking off any excess. Fry for 3–5 minutes on each side until golden and cooked through.

To assemble the sandwiches, spread the mashed avocado on one side of the bread, then top with a little lettuce and slices of tomato and cucumber. Add a spoonful of mango salsa to each, top with the chicken and sandwich together with the remaining bread.

Wrap these stacks in foil and you can even cook them on the barbecue. If the peppers are large, then half on each stack will be more than adequate. We like to serve them with a couple of salads from the counter, but some good, crusty bread and a green salad will be just as good if you are short on time.

AUBERGINE STACKS

1 medium aubergine,
cut into 4 slices

4 thick slices mozzarella

4 large red peppers

Salt and ground black pepper

SERVES 4

Preheat the oven to 180°C/350°F/gas mark 4. Line a baking tray with baking paper. Arrange the aubergine slices in a single layer, then roast for 15–20 minutes, until softened.

Next, hold the peppers over an open flame with tongs and cook until the skin is blackened. Transfer to a bowl, cover with cling film and let sit for 5 minutes before peeling and deseeding.

Put a fresh piece of baking paper on the tray, then assemble each stack by layering slices of aubergine, red pepper, mozeralla and basil leaves, secured together with a wooden skewer soaked in water. Bake in the oven for 10 minutes or until the cheese has melted. Season and serve straight away.

These light, fresh steak fajitas with a zingy, fruity salsa make a great casual lunch. We like them served simply as they are, but feel free to add a dollop of soured cream to cool them down a little if you wish.

SPICED STEAK FAJITAS
WITH TOMATO AND AVOCADO SALSA

Juice of ¼ lime

1 tbsp olive oil

1 tsp chilli flakes

Salt and ground black pepper

600g lean beef rump steak

1 tbsp chopped coriander leaves

1 red onion, peeled, halved and sliced

1 red pepper, seeded and sliced lengthways

1 yellow pepper, seeded and sliced lengthways

8 warmed flour tortillas, to serve

FOR THE AVOCADO AND TOMATO SALSA

1 large avocado, skin and stone removed

Juice of ½ lime

¼ red onion, trimmed, finely sliced

5 cherry tomatoes, quartered

½-1 mild red or green chilli

Salt and ground black pepper

In a shallow dish, combine the lime juice, olive oil, chilli flakes and salt and pepper. Add the steak, turning to coat well. Set aside to marinate for at least 10 minutes.

Meanwhile, place avocado in a bowl. Mash with a fork and add the lime juice, red onion, tomatoes, chilli, salt and pepper. Stir to combine.

Heat a non-stick pan until smoking hot, then add the steak and cook in batches for about 2 minutes on each side for medium rare. Transfer to the plate and cover with foil. Set aside for 5 minutes to rest then cut into slices of about 1cm.

While the steak is resting, wipe the pan clean, put back over a medium-high heat and add the onions and peppers, tossing frequently to prevent burning, for around 3 minutes, until just tender.

To serve, wrap the steak, onions and peppers in the warmed tortillas with a spoonful of the tomato and avocado salsa.

SERVES 4

This is great for lazy summer afternoons or evenings, when you want to eat something fresh and light that still packs a punch. It's a great recipe for a smart barbecue dinner with friends.

PRAWN & SCALLOP SKEWERS
WITH LEMON, CAPER AND OLIVE OIL SALSA

FOR THE SKEWERS

12 large prawns, head and shell removed

12 large scallops

Green salad, to serve

FOR THE MARINADE

400g tin chopped tomatoes

1 garlic clove, crushed

1 bunch basil, roughly chopped

½ tbsp chilli flakes

FOR THE CAPER, LEMON AND OLIVE OIL SALSA

3 tbsp baby capers

2 lemons, zested

1 baby shallot, finely diced

100ml extra virgin olive oil

First make the marinade. In a bowl, mix the chopped tomatoes, garlic, basil and chilli flakes. Add the prawns and scallops and mix well, then allow to marinate for 15 minutes. While it is marinating, soak 4–6 long bamboo skewers in water.

To make the sala, combine all the ingredients in a small bowl, then set aside.

Heat a griddle pan over a high heat, or alternatively preheat your barbecue. Remove the fish from the marinade and thread onto the skewers. Season with salt then griddle or barbecue for around 6 minutes, turning often and basting with the remaining marinade. Place on a serving dish, dress with salsa and serve with a green salad.

SERVES 4

We love our tart of the day. The fillings are always changing according to what looks good at the market. This one is an autumn tart filled with roasted beetroot, mushrooms, spinach and soft, creamy goat's cheese. The secret to success is all in the timing; the tart shell and beetroot can sit around for a bit, but work really hard to get your eggs, mushrooms and spinach all finished at exactly the same time.

WILD MUSHROOM, BEETROOT AND GOAT'S CHEESE TART

4 beetroot, scrubbed, trimmed and cut into wedges

2 tbsp olive oil

12 eggs, beaten

2 sprigs of thyme

250g wild mushrooms, sliced thickly

300g baby spinach

100g goat's cheese, crumbled

salt and ground black pepper

FOR THE PASTRY

250g plain flour

50ml buttermilk

150g unsalted butter, chilled and diced

2 eggs

SERVES 6

To make the pastry, rub the flour and butter together in a bowl until it resembles fine breadcrumbs. Add the buttermilk and stir until it comes together, then add the eggs. As soon as the mixture resembles a dough, roll it into a ball, wrap in cling film and chill for about 15 minutes in the fridge.

Preheat the oven to 180°C/350°F/gas mark 4. On a lightly floured surface, roll out the pastry into a circle about 5mm thick, and wide enough to line the base and sides of a 23cm fluted tart tin. Lay the pastry in the tin and bake for 20 minutes or until golden brown and cooked through. Allow to cool completely.

Whilst the pastry cools, make the filling. Turn up the oven to 190°C/380°F/gas mark 5. Put the beetroot onto a tray, drizzle with olive oil and thyme and cover with foil, then bake for 20 minutes or until beetroot is just tender. Set aside.

Heat a non-stick pan, add the olive oil and eggs with a pinch of salt and black pepper. Stir frequently for about 5 minutes until thick and creamy and still very moist, then set aside. In the same pan, drizzle in a little more olive oil, add the mushrooms and cook for 3–4 minutes until they start to colour. Then add the spinach and cook for a further 1–2 minutes until the spinach has just wilted. Remove from the heat and season.

Pour the eggs and mushrooms into the pastry case. Top with the roasted beetroot and crumble over the goat's cheese. Serve warm or cold, with mixed salad leaves.

Without a doubt this is one of the most luxurious sandwiches you'll ever make, yet it's really quick and easy to put together. We like to serve half-sized versions of this at Summer garden parties, with a glass of champagne or two. If you can't get hold of lobster tails use a whole precooked lobster and begin at step two instead.

LOBSTER ROLLS

2 small uncooked lobster tails (around 250g in total) or 1 precooked lobster.

100g mayonnaise

1 tbsp fresh lemon juice

2 shallots, finely chopped

2 tbsp finely chopped chives

4 brioche rolls, submarine-style if possible

Large handful of watercress, washed

3 tbsp olive oil

SERVES 4

Bring a large saucepan of water to the boil and reduce to a simmer over a medium heat. Poach the lobster tails in their shells for 8–10 minutes or until cooked. Remove them from the pan and set aside to cool, then refrigerate until chilled.

Remove the cooked lobster meat from the shell and dice into 1cm pieces. Combine the mayonnaise, shallots, chives and season to taste. Adjust acidity with the lemon juice as needed.

Preheat the oven to 180°C/350°F/gas mark 4, then pop the brioche rolls in the oven for 2–5 minutes, until crisp and browned.

To assemble, slice the brioche rolls in half and spread 1 tablespoon of the mayonnaise mix on each half. Divide the lobster meat between the rolls, top with some watercress and a little more mayonnaise, then sandwich together and serve immediately.

DESSERTS

DESSERTS

Dessert, in our opinion, can be eaten at any time of
the day, and in the café our tarts, cakes and pies are as
good with a cup of coffee in the morning as they are
with a mint tea after a hearty lunch, although we've
been known to sell a few slices of our chocolate and
walnut marble cake at breakfast!
Seasonality is king though; in autumn our upside down
cake is studded with blackberries, while in summer you
can expect peaches, nectarines and even strawberries.

This classic tart is loved around the world for good reason; crisp, creamy and sharp all in one bite, it's also the perfect make-ahead dessert. The cooked pastry case will keep in an airtight container for 2–3 days, and the crème pâtissière can be made several hours ahead, meaning all you have to do is fold through the cream, fill the case and decorate with raspberries to serve.

SUMMER RASPBERRY TART

FOR THE SWEET SHORTCRUST PASTRY

250g plain flour, sifted

100g icing sugar, sifted

100g unsalted butter, chilled and diced, plus extra to grease the tin

1 tsp vanilla bean paste

2 egg yolks

1–2 tbsp milk, if needed

FOR THE CREME PATISSIERE

500ml whole milk

1 tbsp vanilla bean paste

7 egg yolks

125g caster sugar

60g tbsp cornflour

TO ASSEMBLE

150ml double cream

250g raspberries

1–2 tbsp icing sugar (optional)

SERVES 8

First, make the pastry. Combine the flour, icing sugar and butter in a food processor, then gently pulse the mixture, scraping down the sides of the bowl every so often, until it resembles fine breadcrumbs. Alternatively, put the dry ingredients in a large mixing bowl and rub the pieces of butter into the mix with your hands.

Transfer the mix to a bowl, making a well in the centre. Whisk together the vanilla bean paste with one egg yolk then work this in the flour mixture, adding a little milk if needed. Lightly knead this for a few seconds then shape the dough into a ball, wrap in cling film and chill for at least 30 minutes.

Once the dough has chilled, lightly flour a work surface, then roll out the dough to around 5mm thick, and wide enough to line the base and sides of a 22cm loose-bottomed tart tin. Lay the dough in the tin, gently pressing around the edges, making sure there is a little extra hanging over the edge. Chill again for 1 hour.

Preheat the oven to 180°C/350°F/gas mark 6. Line the pastry case with baking paper, fill with baking beans and cook for 15 minutes until golden brown. Then remove from the oven and discard the beans and baking paper. Whisk together the second egg yolk and 1 tablespoon of milk in a bowl and brush over the pastry then return it to the oven for a further 10–15 minutes. Cool completely on a wire rack.

To make the crème pâtissière, pour 400ml of the milk into a saucepan, stir in the vanilla and then gently heat until almost boiling. Meanwhile, beat the egg yolks and sugar with an electric whisk, then beat in the cornflour and remaining 100ml of milk.

Working quickly, pour the hot milk into the egg mixture, whisking until combined. Return to a clean saucepan, set over a low heat. Whisk continuously until the custard has thickened, around 5 minutes. Remove from the heat, transfer to a bowl and cover with cling film pressed to the surface. Cool to room temperature, then chill in the fridge for 1 hour.

Once the crème pâtissière is cold, whisk the cream to soft peaks then fold through the crème pâtissière until combined. Spoon into the pastry case, smoothing over the top, then dot with the raspberries. Sift over a little icing sugar to serve.

If berries are out of season, try using frozen ones instead, and draining away some of the juice once thawed. Apple, pear and a little lemon zest also work wonderfully in winter months.

MIXED BERRY PIE

FOR THE PASTRY

375g plain flour

2 tbsp caster sugar, plus extra to decorate

¼ tsp salt

175g cold butter, cubed

3 tbsp ice water

2 tsp lemon or lime juice

2 eggs

FOR THE FILLING

50g plain flour

1 tbsp cornflour

pinch of salt

180g caster sugar

1 tsp vanilla extract

½ tsp ground cardamom (optional)

1kg mixed berries (we use a mix of blueberries, raspberries and strawberries)

SERVES 8–10

Mix the flour, sugar and salt in a bowl, then add the butter and rub together until it resembles fine breadcrumbs. Add the water, lemon juice and one egg, and mix until the dough just comes together. Wrap the dough in cling film and chill for at least 30 minutes.

Roll out about two-thirds of the dough on a lightly floured surface then use to line a 24cm tart tin. Wrap up the remaining dough and return it along with the lined tin to the fridge for another 30 minutes.

To make the filling, mix the flour, cornflour, salt, sugar, vanilla and cardamom in a bowl, then add the berries, turning with a large spoon so they are well coated in the mixture.

Preheat oven to 200°C/400°F/gas mark 6. Tip the berry mixture into the pastry case, then unwrap the last of the dough, roll out and cut into long strips to create a lattice pattern. Weave the horizontal strips underneath the vertical ones on a piece of baking paper before carefully sliding it on top of the pie. Whisk the second egg with a little water, then use this to 'glue' the lattice onto the base of the pastry. Pinch the edges together then brush the pie with the rest of the egg wash. Sprinkle some sugar on top.

Bake for 10 minutes, then lower the temperature to 175C/350°F/gas mark 4 and bake for an additional 50–60 minutes or until the filling is bubbling and fragrant. Leave to cool completely before serving with lightly whipped cream or vanilla ice-cream.

These aromatic rolls fly off the counter in the mornings, but warm from the oven, these rolls are good at any time of the day. You can also make the rolls to the point of baking and freeze them, too – just the thing to pull out when someone turns up unexpectedly.

WALNUT ROLLS (MUTAKI)

400g plain flour
½ tsp salt
½ tsp baking powder
½ tsp ground cardamom
200g butter, diced
150g sour cream
3 egg yolks
Icing sugar, to decorate

FOR THE FILLING
150g walnuts
100g caster sugar
3 egg whites
¼ tsp ground cardamom

MAKES 16 ROLLS

In a large bowl or food processor, mix together the flour, salt, baking powder and ground cardamom. Add the butter and pulse until the butter is evenly combined and the mixture resembles fine breadcrumbs. If working by hand, rub the butter into the flour mix with your fingertips until it reaches the desired consistency.

Next, add the egg yolks and sour cream, then mix until it forms a dough. Tip out onto a floured work surface and lightly knead until smooth, then wrap in cling film and chill in the fridge for 30 minutes.

While the dough is resting, make the filling. Tip the walnuts into the food processor, add the sugar, egg whites and cardamom, and pulse to form a rough paste.

Preheat the oven to 200°C/400°F/gas mark 6, then grease and line a couple of baking trays. Remove the dough from the fridge and divide into 2 balls. On a floured work surface, roll each ball into a circle 30cm wide and cut diagonally into 8 triangular pieces. Place a spoonful of the filling at the top of the widest part of each triangle, then roll up towards the tip of the triangle, tucking in the edges of the dough. It will look a bit like a croissant.

Place the rolls on the trays and bake for 30 minutes, until golden. Allow to cool on a wire rack then sprinkle with a little icing sugar.

Feijoa can be difficult to get hold of in the UK, but it's more than worth tracking down to make this sweet, aromatic cake. If you can't find it, try using another tropical fruit such as guava or a very ripe mango.

HONEY FEIJOA CAKE

225g plain flour

1 tsp baking powder

½ tsp bicarbonate of soda

1 tbsp ground almonds

½ tsp salt

225g unsalted butter, softened

4 tbsp full-flavoured honey

225g brown sugar

3 eggs

1 tsp vanilla extract

150g feijoa, mashed

100ml milk

2–3 tbsp flaked almonds, to decorate

Icing sugar, for dusting

SERVES 6–8

Preheat the oven to 170°C/340°F/gas mark 4 and grease and line a 22cm springform cake tin with baking paper.

In a mixing bowl, combine the flours, baking powder, bicarbonate of soda, ground almonds and salt.

In a separate bowl, beat together the butter, honey and sugar with an electric whisk until light and fluffy. Then add the eggs one at a time, beating well after each addition, and the vanilla extract. Next, incorporate two-thirds of the flour mixture and beat until just combined, then add the remaining flour mixture, mashed feijoa and milk, and fold in with a spatula.

Transfer to the prepared tin, spread out the mixture evenly and sprinkle over the flaked almonds. Bake for about 40 minutes until brown on top, then cover loosely with foil and continue baking for another 35 minutes or until a skewer inserted into the middle comes out clean.

Leave to cool in the tin for about 10 minutes and then remove from the tin and dust with icing sugar.

This is one of our favourite cakes on the bakery counter; walnuts, in our opinion, are unsung heroes, but if you only have ground almonds or hazelnuts in the cupboard then they will marry just as well. We also make this with a little splash of cold espresso added to the chocolate batter.

CHOCOLATE AND WALNUT MARBLE CAKE

100g butter, softened

360g caster sugar

4 eggs

250g plain flour

1 tsp baking powder

½ tbsp bicarbonate of soda

200g soured cream

70g ground walnuts

2 tbsp cocoa powder

SERVES 6–8

Preheat the oven to 180°C/350°F/gas mark 4. Grease a 23cm cake tin and line the base with baking paper.

In a bowl, beat the soft butter with half of the sugar using an electric whisk. In a separate bowl, beat the eggs with the rest of the sugar, then add to the butter mix and whisk to make a batter.

Sift together the flour, baking powder and bicarbonate of soda. Mix the soured cream into the batter, then add the flour mix and walnuts. Divide the batter evenly into two bowls. Into one bowl, add the cocoa and mix well.

Put 2 tablespoons of the plain, light coloured batter in the centre of the prepared tin, then add 2 tablespoons of the dark batter in the centre of the light batter. Repeat until the mixtures are used up.

Bake for about 30 minutes then cover the cake with foil and return to the oven for another 20–30 minutes, or until a skewer inserted into the centre comes out clean. Let cool in the tin for 5 minutes, then allow to cool completely on a wire rack.

The sweet, aromatic cardamom syrup is the perfect foil to the sharp redcurrants in these moreish muffins.

REDCURRANT MUFFINS

150g redcurrants

10ml cardamom syrup

130g caster sugar, plus extra for sprinkling

50g unsalted butter

375g self-raising flour

2 medium eggs, beaten

140ml milk

30g flaked almonds, plus extra for sprinkling

Icing sugar, for dusting

MAKES 12

Preheat the oven to 200°C/400°F/gas mark 6. Line a 12-hole muffin tin with paper cases. Place the redcurrants in a bowl and drizzle the cardamom syrup over them, stirring gently to make sure they are well coated.

In a bowl, beat together the sugar and butter with an electric whisk until light and fluffy. Add the eggs with the whisk speed on low, then once incorporated, add half of the flour, the milk and finally the rest of the flour. Beat until only just combined, then gently fold through the almonds and redcurrants.

Spoon the mixture into muffin cases and top with extra flaked almonds. Bake for 20–30 minutes, until risen and golden. Transfer to a wire rack to cool and serve warm or at room temperature with a little dusting of icing sugar.

Our loaf cakes are extremely popular mid-morning, and this one with sweet but sharp physalis is one of our customers' favourites. It will keep well in an airtight tin for 3–4 days.

PHYSALIS AND YOGHURT LOAF CAKE

150g unsalted butter, melted

220g caster sugar

3 eggs

140g Greek-style yoghurt

Zest and juice of 1 lemon

1 tsp vanilla extract

225g self-raising flour, sifted

250g physalis, leaves removed and halved, plus extra to serve

Icing sugar, for dusting

SERVES 6–8

Preheat oven to 160°C/325F/gas mark 3 and grease and line a 500g loaf tin. Place the butter, sugar, eggs, yoghurt, lemon zest and vanilla in a bowl and whisk to combine. Add the flour and whisk againuntil well mixed.

Fold the physalis through the batter and pour into the prepared tin. Smooth the surface with a spatula and bake the cake for about 1 hour or until a skewer inserted into the centre comes out clean. Allow the loaf to cool in the tin for 10 minutes before turning it out onto a wire rack to cool completely. Dust with icing sugar and top with extra physalis to serve.

We make this tart in a 36cm rectangular tin then slice into bars, but it will work in a round 23cm tart tin too.

FIG TART

2 egg yolks

50g caster sugar

25g plain flour

250ml milk

vanilla pod, cut open

2 tbsp double cream

9 fresh figs

Icing sugar, for dusting

FOR THE PASTRY

225g plain flour, sifted

½ tsp salt

100g unsalted butter, chilled and diced

130ml cold water

SERVES 6–8

First, make the pastry. Mix the flour and salt in a large bowl, then, using your fingertips, rub the butter into the flour until it resembles fine breadcrumbs. Add the water and mix to form a dough. Turn out onto a lightly floured surface and gently knead until smooth. Wrap in cling film and place in the fridge for 20 minutes to rest.

Meanwhile, mix together the egg yolks and sugar for 1 minute, then add the flour and stir to incorporate. Heat the milk and vanilla pod in a saucepan until almost boiling, then slowly stir into the egg and flour mixture. Return to the saucepan and cook over a medium heat until it thickens. Return to the bowl, whisk for 10 seconds and allow to cool.

Preheat the oven to 200°C/400°F/gas mark 6. On a lightly floured surface roll out the pastry into a 3mm thick rectangle, large enough to line a 12 x 36cm rectangular tin. Line the tin with the pastry, gently pressing into the sides to fit. Trim the edges and prick the base with a fork, then line with baking paper and fill with baking beans. Bake for about 20 minutes then remove the paper and beans and bake for another 20 minutes, until pale golden. Remove the tart from the oven and allow to cool in the tin.

Mix the cream into the cooled custard and spread over the base of the pastry. Cut the figs into quarters and arrange on top of the custard, then dust with icing sugar before slicing and serving.

Although lemon meringue pie is a classic for good reason, this tropical version will win hands down at any dinner table. Fragrant and sweet, the gentle sharpness of passionfruit feels like a more harmonious marriage for the Italian meringue topping. It can be made as one large tart, or little individual tartlets as shown here.

PASSIONFRUIT MERINGUE TART

FOR THE CURD

5 large eggs

200g sugar

1 tbsp cornflour

Small pinch of salt

12 passionfruit, halved

110g unsalted butter, cubed

FOR THE PASTRY

450g plain flour,
plus additional for dusting

2 tbsp sugar

A pinch of salt

250g butter

1 large egg yolk

1 ½ tbsp ice cold water

FOR THE MERINGUE

4 large egg whites,
room temperature

Pinch of salt

150g sugar

4 tbsp water

SERVES 6–8

First, make the passionfruit curd. Whisk the eggs, sugar, cornflour and salt in a bowl. Strain the passionfruit through a sieve to collect the juice, then heat this in a pan until simmering. Incorporate the hot juice into the egg mixture, a tablespoon at a time, whisking constantly. Return this to the pan over a medium heat and whisk in the butter, cube by cube. Keep whisking as the curd begins to boil and thickens, for up to 10 minutes. Allow to cool a little, then pour into a bowl. Cover with cling film and chill in the fridge for at least 8 hours or overnight.

When the curd has nearly chilled, make the pastry. Whisk the flour, sugar and salt in a mixing bowl, then rub in the butter until it resembles fine breadcrumbs. Lightly whisk the egg yolk and water, then pour into the flour mixture and combine to form a dough. Add a little more water if necessary but don't overwork it. Wrap in cling film and chill for 1 hour.

On a lightly floured surface roll the pastry out into a 30cm circle and use to line a 25cm fluted tart tin, gently pressing into the sides to fit. Trim the edges and prick the base with a fork then return to the fridge for another 30 minutes. Preheat the oven to 180°C/350°F/gas mark 4. Line the pastry case with baking paper and fill with baking beans. Bake for about 20 minutes then remove the paper and beans and bake for another 20 minutes, until pale golden. Leave to cool in the tin.

Meanwhile, make the meringue. Using a mixer, whisk the egg whites and salt to soft peaks. Boil the sugar and the water over a medium heat to dissolve the sugar and make a syrup. Allow to cool slightly, then with the mixer on a medium speed, carefully pour the hot syrup into the eggs, in a slow, thin stream down the side of the bowl. Increase the mixer speed to high and beat until the meringue is glossy and holds stiff peaks, around 10–15 minutes.

To assemble, spread the curd evenly in the pastry case then pipe or spoon on the meringue, forming small peaks. Toast the top with a small blow torch or place under a hot grill, until the meringues start to turn a light brown. Slice and serve.

This cake is perfect for summer parties – a real show-stopper for reasonably little effort. If it's for a special occasion, try decorating with a few flowers and lightly dusting with icing sugar as well as berries for a rustic but chic look.

BERRY & LEMON CAKE
WITH CREAM CHEESE FROSTING

230g unsalted butter, softened
to room temperature

250g caster sugar

100g light brown sugar

4 eggs

1 tbsp vanilla extract

360g plain flour

½ tsp salt

1 tbsp baking powder

200ml buttermilk

Zest and juice of 2 lemons

150g blackberries,
plus extra to decorate

150g blueberries,
plus extra to decorate

FOR THE CREAM CHEESE
FROSTING

225g full-fat cream cheese

120g unsalted butter

400g icing sugar

2 tbsp double cream

1 tsp vanilla extract

SERVES 10–12

Preheat the oven to 180°C/350°F/gas mark 4, then grease and line three 20cm cake tins. Beat the butter and both types of sugar together with an electric whisk until pale and fluffy, then add the eggs and vanilla and continue beating for a further 2 minutes.

In a large bowl, sift together the flour, salt and baking powder. Slowly add the dry ingredients to the butter mixture, beating with the electric whisk as you go, then add the buttermilk, lemon zest and lemon juice. Beat briefly with a wooden spoon until everything is combined. Stir the berries through the batter, being careful not to overmix, then divide the batter evenly between the prepared cake tins.

Bake for 20 minutes, or until a skewer inserted in the centre comes out clean. Allow to cool in the tins for a couple of minutes then turn out onto a wire rack to cool completely.

Meanwhile, prepare the frosting. Beat the cream cheese and butter together until light and smooth, then add the icing sugar, cream and vanilla extract, beating until incorporated.

To assemble the cake, place one sponge on a serving plate, then evenly cover the top with cream cheese frosting. Place the next sponge on top, then cover with more frosting. Add the third layer, top with more frosting then decorate with the extra blackberries and blueberries. Chill for 45 minutes before serving.

As soon as we discovered this cheat's cheesecake, we were hooked; never will there be a better dessert for those moments when your willpower is challenged by the need for a little indulgence.

CHEESECAKE STUFFED STRAWBERRIES

24 large strawberries, hulled

230g cream cheese, brought up to room temperature

60g icing sugar

1 tsp vanilla extract

24 small blueberries

SERVES 4–6

Trim the leaf end of the strawberries,so they can sit cut-side down. Using a small knife, cut a deep 'X' from the tip down on each, being careful not to cut all the way through.

Beat the cream cheese, icing sugar and vanilla in a bowl with an electric whisk until smooth and fluffy.

Gently open up each strawberry and pipe the filling inside using a pastry bag or zip-top bag with a small star piping tip. If you don't have the piping tools, just cut off the corner of a zip-top bag and squeeze the cheesecake filling inside the strawberries that way. Top each filled strawberry with a blueberry.

These are best served after the strawberries have been chilled for at least an hour, and they will keep in the fridge for 2–3 days.

This pretty cake is just as good served warm with a little soured cream for dessert as it is eaten in the afternoon with a strong cup of tea. It will keep for 3–4 days in an airtight container.

BLACKBERRY ALMOND UPSIDE DOWN CAKE

400g fresh blackberries

125g plain flour

1 tsp baking powder

½ tsp bicarbonate of soda

30g ground almonds

125g unsalted butter, softened to room temperature

250g caster sugar

1–2 tsp finely grated lemon zest

1 tsp vanilla extract

4 eggs

125ml natural yoghurt or buttermilk

SERVES 8

Preheat oven to 170°C/340°F/gas mark 4. Grease and line a 23cm round cake tin with baking paper. Tightly arrange the blackberries in the bottom of the tin.

Mix the flour, baking powder, bicarbonate of soda and ground almonds in a large mixing bowl.

Place the butter, sugar, lemon zest and vanilla extract in another bowl and beat with an electric whisk for about 8–10 minutes or until pale and creamy. Add the eggs, one at a time, until incorporated. With the whisk on a low speed, add the dry ingredients in three additions, alternating with the yoghurt.

Spoon the batter into the tin and smooth the top. Bake for 35 minutes, or until a skewer inserted into the centre comes out clean. Allow to cool for 15 minutes in the tin, then invert the cake onto a serving plate and remove the tin and paper carefully. Allow to cool a little, then serve.

A cross between a croissant and a muffin, cruffins fly off the counter when we serve them fresh from the oven. You should definitely try all four variations before picking your favourite; they are more than worth the effort.

CRUFFINS FOUR WAYS

350ml milk

55g caster sugar

14g dried yeast

500g plain flour

2 tsp salt

350g cold unsalted butter

NUTELLA AND
MACADAMIA

12 tsp Nutella spread
handful of roughly
chopped macadamias

DULCE DE LECHE

12 tsp dulce de leche
icing sugar to dust

CARAMEL POPCORN

12 tsp caramel
handful of popcorn

LYCHEE AND ROSE

6 tbsp fresh smashed lycees
sprinkle of rose water

MAKES 12

Heat the milk in a saucepan over a low heat until lukewarm, then transfer to a large bowl with the sugar and yeast and stir to combine. Add the flour and salt, then knead for around 5 minutes to form a soft, sticky dough, adding more flour if necessary. Shape the dough into a rough rectangle, wrap in cling film and chill for 1 hour. Pound the butter with a rolling pin to soften to a similar consistency as the dough, then place between sheets of baking paper and roll out to a 20cm x 15cm rectangle. Chill in the fridge until needed.

On a lightly floured surface, roll out the dough to a 45cm x 25cm rectangle. Place the butter in the centre of dough with the long sides of one rectangle parallel to short sides of the other. Fold the long sides of dough over the butter then the short sides, so the butter is fully enclosed. Flatten the dough slightly, then roll out again to a 45cm x 25cm strip running along the worktop. Fold the left third of the pastry over itself, then fold the right third over the top to make a rectangle 15cm wide. Wrap in cling film and chill for another hour. Repeat this folding and chilling process three more times to create a laminated dough, then wrap in cling film and return to the fridge for 8–12 hours, or overnight.

Remove the dough from the fridge and roll out into a 45cm long strip. Roll up lengthways into a long, tight log then divide into 12 pieces. Spoon a teaspoon of filling in the centre of each piece. Arrange the cruffins 5cm apart on two oven trays lined with baking paper, then cover lightly with cling film and leave to rise in a warm place for another hour.

Meanwhile, preheat the oven to 220°C/440°F/gas mark 7. Spray water inside the oven to create steam, reduce the heat to 200°C/400°F/gas mark 6 and bake the cruffins for 20-25 minutes or until a deep golden colour, swapping and turning the trays halfway through. Transfer to a wire rack to cool for 10 minutes, then top with the final flavourings and serve.

FROM THE BAKERY

Being based in Kensignton, central London,
weekdays at Brown and Rosie's are wonderfully
buzzy, with everyone from busy commuters looking
for breakfast on the go to tourists wanting a leisurely
coffee and cake to set them up for the day.
Our bakery counter, packed with fresh-from-the-
oven bakes, showcases the ethos of our café; quality
and variety. From simple yoghurt cakes and seasonal
muffins to spiced buns and pastries, there's plenty to
choose from; we make sure our bestseller, fragrant
walnut rolls, never run out though.

At Brown and Rosie's we make our sourdough fresh every day. The loaf we make here is a simpler version intended for the home baker.

SOURDOUGH BREAD

FOR THE STARTER

200g strong white bread flour

1 tsp easy-blend dried yeast

250ml cold water

FOR THE BREAD

400g strong white bread flour

1 tsp easy-blend dried yeast

2 tsp salt

225ml water

MAKES 1 LOAF

First make the starter. Combine the flour and yeast in a bowl, then mix in the water. Cover with cling film and leave to stand at room temperature for 24 hours.

To make the bread, combine the flour, yeast and salt, then make a well in the centre. Add in the starter mixture and the water and bring together to form a dough. Tip out onto a floured work surface and knead for about 10 minutes until the dough is smooth and elastic. Place in a clean, oiled bowl, cover with oiled cling film and leave to rise for 1 hour, or until doubled in size.

Tip the dough onto a floured work surface and shape into an oval. Dust a baking sheet with flour and place the loaf on top. Cover with a tea towel and leave to rise for another hour until doubled in size again.

Preheat the oven to 220°C/440°F/gas mark 7. Place a roasting pan on the shelf at the bottom and add 250ml cold water. Slash the top of the loaf with a sharp knife, then put the loaf on the middle rack and bake for about 25 minutes until golden and the loaf sounds hollow when tapped underneath. Transfer to a wire rack to cool.

You'll need to make the simple starter for this loaf a couple of days in advance, but it requires hardly any effort. We love to serve this loaf with our daily soups, but it's also the perfect accompaniment to a plate of meat and cheese.

KALAMATA OLIVE AND HERBED PROVENCE BREAD

FOR THE RYE SOURDOUGH STARTER

200g stoneground rye flour

350ml buttermilk

FOR THE BREAD

300ml lukewarm water

20g fresh yeast

200g strong white bread flour, plus extra for dusting

150g wholegrain stoneground spelt flour

1 tsp salt

50g kalamata olives

2 tbsp thyme leaves

2 tbsp marjoram leaves

2 tbsp oregano leaves

1 tsp rosemary leaves

1 tsp dried lavender

First make the starter. Combine the flour and buttermilk in a bowl, then put into an airtight container and leave to stand at room temperature for 2 days.

When the starter is ready, put it together with the water in a mixing bowl, crumble in the yeast and whisk to combine. Then add the flours and salt and mix well; the dough will be pretty sticky. Cover the bowl with cling film and chill in the fridge for 8 hours.

When the dough is ready, tip out onto a floured work surface and knead for a few minutes, then add the olives and herbs and shape into a round loaf. Place on a lined baking sheet then cover with a tea towel and leave to rise in a warm place for 30 minutes.

Meanwhile heat the oven to 240°C/480°F/gas mark 9. When the bread is risen, slash a cross in the top of the loaf with a sharp knife. Spray cold water in the oven to create a little steam, then bake the loaf for about 30 minutes until golden and crisp. Transfer to a wire rack to cool.

MAKES 1 LOAF

We use this loaf for a lot of our sandwiches in the café.
Vary the seeds depending on what you have in the cupboard,
or tweak the flour ratios if you like a lighter or darker rye loaf.

THREE-SEED RYE BREAD

18g fresh yeast

300ml lukewarm water

300g dark rye flour

75g wholemeal flour

75g strong white bread flour

1 tsp salt

70g linseeds,
plus extra for top

70g pumpkin seeds,
plus extra for top

70g sunflower seeds,
plus extra for top

1 tbsp barley malt syrup

MAKES 1 LOAF

Crumble the yeast into the warmed water and stir until dissolved. In a large bowl, mix together all of the flour, the salt, linseeds, pumpkin seeds and sunflower seeds. Add the barley malt syrup and yeast mixture, stirring until you have a smooth dough.

Tip the dough out onto a lightly floured work surface and knead for 5–10 minutes, until smooth and elastic. Return the dough to the bowl and cover with a tea towel. Leave in a warm place for 1–2 hours to rise until doubled in size.

Once risen, knead the bread lightly to knock back for a few seconds, then roughly shape the dough into a loaf and place on a greased and lined baking sheet. Brush the top with water and sprinkle over more seeds, then cover with the tea towel again and leave to rise for another 30 minutes in a warm place.

Preheat the oven to 220°C/400°F/gas mark 6. When the second proving is complete, cut a few diagonal slashes across the top of the loaf with a sharp knife. Bake the loaf for about 45 minutes until golden; the loaf should sound hollow when you tap the base. Transfer to a wire rack to cool.

This bread is as good for breakfast, thickly sliced and toasted with a generous spoonful of marmalade, as it is served with cheese and meats for a relaxed lunch. This loaf freezes well, and will keep in an airtight tin for a couple of days.

SPELT, WALNUT, RAISIN AND FIG BREAD

20g fresh yeast

350ml lukewarm water

150–200g strong white flour, plus extra for dusting

50g butter, softened

5g salt

300g wholegrain spelt flour

1 tbsp honey or dark treacle

75g dried figs, roughly chopped

75g raisins

75g walnuts, roughly chopped

1 beaten egg, for brushing

1 tsp caraway seeds

MAKES 1 LOAF

Crumble the yeast into a bowl with the warm water, add 50g of the white flour and mix well, then set aside.

In a separate bowl, mix the butter, salt and rest of the flour, then stir in the yeast mixture and honey. Bring together into a dough then tip out and knead on a lightly floured surface for about 10 minutes. Put into a lightly oiled bowl, cover with a tea towel and leave it to rise for 1 hour.

Tip the dough onto a floured work surface, incorporate the fruit and nuts into the dough then divide into two equal pieces. Shape into your desired loaf, then cover with the tea towel and leave to rise again in a warm place for another hour.

Preheat the oven to 180°C/350°F/gas mark 4. With a sharp knife, slash the top of the bread, then brush with beaten egg and scatter with caraway seeds. Spray cold water into the oven to create steam, then bake the loaf for about 35 minutes, until risen and browned. Leave to cool in the tin for about 10 minutes before turning out onto a wire rack to cool.

This is a really unusual and unique type of savoury pastry, filled with minced beef and topped with the sweet and sour combination of icing sugar and sumac. Originating from Azerbaijan, it might sound a bit crazy but we promise you, they taste phenomenal!

CHUDU

FOR PASTRY

1 tbsp dried yeast

100ml lukewarm water

230ml lukewarm buttermilk

2 tbsp sugar

400g flour

½ tsp salt

200g butter

1 egg

FOR THE FILLING

1 tsp extra virgin olive oil

1 onion, finely chopped

450g beef mince

Salt and ground black pepper

2 tsp fresh oregano leaves, chopped

TO DECORATE

1 egg, beaten

2 tsp sumac

2 tsp icing sugar

MAKES 12

Sprinkle the yeast into the water and buttermilk, whisk to combine, then add the sugar and 50g of the flour, and mix well. In a separate mixing bowl, mix together the remaining flour and salt then rub in the butter with your fingertips, until it resembles breadcrumbs.

Mix the egg into the yeast mixture then incorporate this into the flour mixture to form a dough. Tip out and knead lightly on a floured work surface. Divide the dough into 12 balls, flatten into discs and place on a floured baking tray. Cover with cling film and chill for 2–3 hours.

Meanwhile, prepare the filling. Put the oil in a frying pan over a medium heat, then add the onion and cook until it begins to soften. Add the mince, oregano and a generous amount of salt and pepper and cook for 20 minutes. Remove from the heat and leave to cool.

Preheat the oven to 200°C/400°F/gas mark 6. On a floured work surface, roll out the discs of dough into thinner circles 15cm wide and 3mm thick. Put a spoonful of the filling into the centre of each disc, then fold the edges into the centre, overlapping and pressing the edges closed firmly with your fingertips to seal the chudu.

Arrange the chudu on a baking tray lined with baking paper and brush with the beaten egg. Mix together the icing sugar and sumac and sprinkle over the pastries. Bake for 20–30 minutes until golden, then transfer to a wire rack to cool a little before serving warm.

These raisin and buttermilk buns are delicious served on their own, warm from the oven or even with a little butter and your favourite jam.

RAISIN AND BUTTERMILK BUNS

300g strong white bread flour

75g caster sugar

½ tsp salt

5g fast-action dried yeast

100g raisins

200ml lukewarm buttermilk

2 eggs: 1 whole,
1 beaten for the glaze

100g butter, melted

MAKES 12

In a large bowl, mix the flour, sugar, salt, yeast and raisins, then make a well in the centre.

In a jug, mix the buttermilk with the whole egg and melted butter, then pour into the centre of the flour and mix to form a dough. Tip out onto a lightly floured work surface and knead for 5–10 minutes, until smooth and elastic. Put the dough in a lightly greased bowl, cover with a tea towel and leave to rise in a warm place for 1 hour, or until double the size.

Once risen, divide the dough into 12 pieces, then roll into smooth balls. Line a 12-hole muffin tray with paper cases and put a dough ball in each case, then cover again with the tea towel and allow to rise in a warm place for a further 20–30 minutes.

Preheat the oven to 180°C/350°F/gas mark 4. Brush the buns with the beaten egg and bake for about 15–20 minutes, until risen and golden. Transfer to a wire rack to cool.

JUICES AND SMOOTHIES

Whether you want a quick invigorating health boost or a long, refreshing summer cooler, we've got it covered. At Brown and Rosie's, we like to use as many organic ingredients as possible and always make our juices just before serving to achieve the maximum vitamin and nutrient hit. Our sweet and creamy smoothies can be a pick-me-up, a wake-me-up or just a good old comfort fix without any guilt attached. Rena is a purist and likes a simple fruit hit with none of the fancy stuff, while Leyli just can't help herself once the blender's out and likes to put anything and everything in hers!

With today's busy lifestyles, we need a simple and effective way to nourish our bodies and restore a state of wellbeing. Our natural juices are squeezed full of superfoods like kale, ginger and beetroot that are packed with vitamins, nutrients and antioxidants; they provide an instant health kick and allow our bodies and minds to function at their highest levels.

JUICES

VEGGIE GARDEN

3cm piece fresh ginger, peeled

1 beetroot, trimmed and cut into wedges

4 carrots, peeled and trimmed

25g parsley

Press the ginger, beetroot, carrots and parsley through the juicer. Pour into a glass and serve.

SERVES 1

KALE ESCAPE

2 large handfuls of kale leaves

1 celery stick

2 apples, cored and cut into wedges

¼ cucumber

Press the kale, celery, apple and cucumber through the juicer. Pour into a glass and serve.

SERVES 1

IRON MAN

2 apples, cored and cut into wedges

150g pineapple, peeled and cored

1 orange, peeled

4 mint leaves, plus extra to serve

Press the apples, pineapple, orange and mint through the juicer. Pour into a glass, and decorate with fresh mint leaves, if liked.

SERVES 1

BEACH HOUSE

½ mango, peeled, stone removed and chopped

4 large strawberries, hulled

1 passionfruit

¼ watermelon, about 300g, rind removed

Press the mango, strawberries, passionfruit and watermelon through the juicer. Pour into a glass and serve.

SERVES 1

Our refreshing waters with hint of vitamin-rich citrus offer a great health boost to start the day. Whether you add orange, peach or cucumber, these vitamin waters will keep you hydrated and flush any toxins from your system. If you prefer a fizz, then choose a naturally sparkling water.

HEALTHY VITAMIN WATER

BASIC CITRUS

1 orange
½ grapefruit
1 lemon

PEACH *AND* VANILLA

1 peach
2 vanilla pods
1 pinch of stevia

MINT, CUCUMBER *AND* LIME

1 Lebanese cucumber
1 lime
a handful of mint leaves

Wash all the fruit and vegetables and scrub any citrus fruit thoroughly, then slice up into roughly equal sized pieces. Place in a pitcher with any remaining ingredients and mix together to release some of the juices. Fill the pitcher with cold water, stir and then leave in the fridge overnight to infuse before serving.

MAKES 1 PITCHER

Every now and again we all need to press the reset button so we've made detoxing simple with our fresh and nutritious smoothie blends. Guaranteed to leave you feeling motivated and energised, these are our go-to recipes but feel free to experiment and add in your favourite fruits too!

SMOOTHIES

PASSION AND MANGO

1 banana, peeled

1 passionfruit

Organic Raw honey, to taste

1 mango,
peeled and stone removed

3 tbsp low-fat yoghurt

Put all the ingredients in a blender and blend well until smooth. Check the consistency and add a little water to thin to your liking. Pour into a glass and serve.

SERVES 1

ORGANIC BANANA AND CINNAMON

2 bananas, peeled

½ tsp cinnamon

½–1 tsp organic raw honey

225ml almond milk

Put all the ingredients in a blender and blend well until smooth. Pour into a glass and dust over a little more cinnamon to serve.

SERVES 1–2

ORGANIC SUPER BERRY

Handful of blueberries
and raspberries

1 tsp acai powder

1 tbsp goji berries

1 tbsp chia seeds

1 tsp organic raw honey

100ml pure coconut water

Put all the ingredients in a blender
and blend until smooth. Pour into a
glass and serve.

SERVES 1

WHOLE FOOD SMOOTHIE

1 handful kale leaves

1 green apple,
cored and cut into wedges

½ avocado

3 fresh feijoa or kiwi fruit

1 tbsp chai seeds

1 tsp organic honey

1 tsp desiccated coconut

3–4 ice cubes

almond milk (optional)

Put all the ingredients in a blender
and process until smooth and creamy.
Check the consistency and add a little
almond milk to thin to your liking. Pour
into a glass and serve.

SERVES 1

INDEX

Aioli, Crab Bruschetta with Lime **65**, 67
almonds *9*
    Blackberry Almond Upside Down Cake **216,** 217
    Honey-Baked Granola **26**, 27, *39*
apples, in juices and smoothies 242, 243, 249
apricots 140
asparagus
    and Halloumi Salad **84**, 86
    Omelette with Roasted Asparagus 58, **59**
aubergines
    Black Rice, Kale and Aubergine Salad **85**, 87
    Stacks **175**, 177
avocados *15*, 178, 249
    Chicken Sandwich with Mango and Avocado **174**, 176
    Crab Bruschetta with Crushed Avocado **65**, 67
    Fresh Herbed Ricotta with Kumato, Avocado and Grapes **64**, 66
    Tomato and Avocado Salsa 178, **179**
    Yoghurt 150, **151**

bananas
    and Cinnamon Smoothie **246**, 248
    leaves 150, **151**, 158, **159**
    and Peach Waffles **34**, 35
Basic Citrus Water 244, **245**
basil *12*, 107
Beach House (juice) **241**, 243
beans *10*, 157
beef
    and Basil Salad **106**, 107
    mince 144, **145**, **232**, 233
    Rib with Herby Cannellini Bean Spread **156**, 157
    Skirt Steak with Chimichurri Sauce and Salsa **138**, 139
    Spiced Steak Fajitas with Tomato and Avocado Salsa 178, **179**
    Steak Sandwich with Red Pepper Relish 166, **167**
    Stew with Mint and Sour Plums **142**, 143
beetroot
    Roasted Beetroot, Pecan and Feta Salad **96**, 97
    Salad with Yuzu Dressing 102, **103**
    Spread **70**, 71
    Veggie Garden (juice) **240**, 242
    Wild Mushroom, Beetroot and Goat's Cheese Tart 182, **183**
berries *15*, *17*, 191 *see also* blueberries; cranberries

Cherries on Brioche 36, **37**
    and Lemon Cake **212**, 213
    Mixed Berry Pie 192, **193**
    Organic Super Berry Smoothie **247**, 249
    Raspberry Tart **190**, 191
Bircher Muesli 24, **25**
Black Pepper Crab with Ginger 128, **129**
Black Rice, Kale and Aubergine Salad **85**, 87
Blackberry Almond Upside Down Cake **216**, 217
blueberries 24, 28
    Fluffy Pikelets with Blueberries 32, **33**
breads *see also* brioche; sourdough
    Kalamata Olive and Herbed Provence Bread **226**, 227
    Lobster Rolls 184, **185**
    Pulled Pork Sliders **168**, 169
    Raisin and Buttermilk Buns 234, **235**
    Sourdough Bread **224**, 225
    Spelt, Walnut, Raisin and Fig Bread **229**, 231
    Three-Seed Rye Bread **228**, 230
brioche 184
    Cherries on Brioche 36, **37**
Buns, Raisin and Buttermilk 234, **235**
Butternut Squash Soup **99**, 101

cabbage 170
    Slaw **168**, 169
cakes
    Berry and Lemon Cake **212**, 213
    Blackberry Almond Upside Down Cake **216**, 217
    Chocolate and Walnut Marble Cake **200**, 201
    Herb Cake 132, **133**
    Honey Feijoa Cake 198, **199**
    Physalis and Yoghurt Loaf Cake **203**, 205
Cannellini Bean Spread **156**, 157
Caper, Lemon and Olive Oil Salsa **180**, 181
cardamom *14*, 197, 204
carrots 161, 170
Cashew Cream **110**, 111
Cauliflower and Tahini Salad **92**, 93
Ceviche, Tuna **82**, 83
cheese 177, 213
    feta 88, 97
    goat's cheese 173, 182
    Poached Chicken and Stracchino Salad 76, **77**
    ricotta 66, 125
Cheesecake Stuffed Strawberries 214, **215**

Cherries on Brioche 36, **37**
chestnuts *9*, 140
    Chicken with Chestnuts and Redcurrants 136, **137**
chia seeds *10*, 24
    Coconut Chia Pudding 28, **29**
chicken
    with Chestnuts and Redcurrants 136, **137**
    Poached Chicken and Stracchino Salad 76, **77**
    Sandwich with Mango and Avocado **174**, 176
Chimichurri Sauce **138**, 139
Chocolate and Walnut Marble Cake **200**, 201
Chorizo, Soft-Baked Eggs with Kale and **60**, 61
Chudu **232**, 233
Cinnamon and Organic Banana Smoothie **246**, 248
Citrus Water 244, **245**
coconut *11*, *15*
    Chia Pudding 28, **29**
coleslaw **168**, 169
coriander *12*, 100, 139
courgettes
    Fritters with Herby Yoghurt **52**, 54
    Stuffed Courgette Flowers **124**, 125
crab
    Black Pepper Crab with Ginger 128, **129**
    Bruschetta **65**, 67
cranberries 43
    Wild Rice with Cranberries 140, **141**
Crayfish Salad **98**, 100
Crème pâtissière **190**, 191
Cruffins Four Ways 218, **219**
Cucumber, Mint and Lime Water 244, **245**
Curd, Passionfruit **210**, 211
Cuttlefish with Rice and Tomatoes 148, **149**

Dill-Cured Salmon 62, **63**
dressings, salad *11*, 111
    for Beef and Basil Salad **106**, 107
    for Cauliflower and Tahini Salad **92**, 93
    for Crayfish Salad **98**, 100
    Lemon Fennel Seed Dressing 76, **77**
    for Quail with Radicchio and Golden Raisins **118**,119
    for Roasted Beetroot, Pecan and Feta Salad **96**, 97
    for Seared Tuna Salad **78**, 79
    for Steak Sandwich with Red Pepper Relish 166,
        167
    Truffle Dressing **152**, 153
    for Warm Smoked Rainbow Trout Salad 108, **109**
    Yuzu Dressing 102, **103**
Duck with Quinoa and Pomegranate **152**, 153

eggs *9*
    Herb Cake 132, **133**
    Herbed Lentils with Grilled Polenta and Poached
        Egg 68, **69**

Omelette with Roasted Asparagus 58, **59**
    'Our Healthy Breakfast Plate' 70, 71
    Portobello Mushrooms, Poached Egg and Hummus
        on Sourdough **48**, 49
    Soft-Baked Eggs with Kale and Chorizo **60**, 61
    Soft-Fried Eggs with Green and Red Salsa 50, **51**
Elderflower & Berry Yoghurt 36, **37**

Fajitas, Spiced Steak 178, **179**
feijoa *17*, 249
    Feijoa Spread 40, **41**
    Honey Feijoa Cake 198, **199**
fennel
    Lemon Fennel Seed Dressing 76, **77**
    Salmon and Fennel with Horseradish Spread **53**, 55
feta cheese
    Roasted Beetroot, Pecan and Feta Salad **96**, 97
    Watermelon and Feta Salad 88, **89**
figs
    Caramelised Figs with Yoghurt **38**, 39
    Fig, Walnut, Prosciutto and Pomegranate Salad
        110, 111
    Spelt, Walnut, Raisin and Fig Bread **229**, 231
    Tart 208, **209**
Fluffy Pikelets with Blueberries 32, **33**
Fragrant Butternut Squash Soup **99**, 101
Fresh Herbed Ricotta with Kumato, Avocado and
    Grapes **64**, 66
Frosting, Cream Cheese **212**, 213
fruits *see* berries

ginger *14*, 242
    Black Pepper Crab with Ginger 128, **129**
goji berries 27, 249
granola
    Bars **42**, 43
    Honey-Baked Granola **26**, 27, *39*
Grapes, Fresh Herbed Ricotta with Kumato, Avocado
    and **64**, 66
Green Papaya Salad 94, **95**
Green Salsa 50, **51**
Grilled Herby Lamb with Baby Cherry Tomatoes 116,
    117
Guinea Fowl with Quince 122, **123**

Halloumi and Asparagus Salad **84**, 86
hazelnuts 158
Healthy Breakfast Plate 70, 71
Healthy Vitamin Water 244, **245**
herbs *11–12*
    Herb Cake 132, **133**
    Fresh Herbed Ricotta **64**, 66
    Grilled Herby Lamb with Baby Cherry Tomatoes 116,
        117

Kalamata Olive and Herbed Provence Bread **226**, 227

Lentils with Grilled Polenta 68, **69**

Roast Beef Rib with Herby Cannellini Bean Spread **156**, 157

Yoghurt 52, 54, **160**, 161

honey *17*, 24, 32

Honey-Baked Granola 26, 27, *39*

Honey Feijoa Cake 198, **199**

Horseradish Spread **53**, 55

hummus 49

Sweet Potato Hummus **130**, 131

icing, Cream Cheese Frosting **212**, 213

Iron Man (juice) **241**, 243

juices **240–1**, 242–3

kale 242, 249

Black Rice, Kale and Aubergine Salad **85**, 87

Soft-Baked Eggs with Kale and Chorizo **60**, 61

Kumato, Avocado and Grapes, Fresh Herbed Ricotta with **64**, 66

lamb

Grilled Herby Lamb with Baby Cherry Tomatoes 116, **117**

Slow-Roasted Leg of Lamb with Rainbow Carrots and Herb Yoghurt **160**, 161

lemons 244

Berry and Lemon Cake **212**, 213

Lemon, Caper and Olive Oil Salsa **180**, 181

Lemon Fennel Seed Dressing 76, **77**

Lentils with Grilled Polenta 68, **69**

lettuce 83

Lime Aioli **65**, 67

Lobster Rolls 184, **185**

mangoes 27, 243, 248

Chicken Sandwich with Mango and Avocado **174**, 176

Maple Syrup, Spiced **34**, 35

marinades

for beef **106**, 107

for lamb 116, **160**, 161

for pork 150, **151**

for poultry 119, 176

for Prawn and Scallop Skewers **180**, 181

Meringue Tart, Passionfruit **210**, 211

mint *12–14*, 143, 244

Mixed Berry Pie 192, **193**

mozzarella 177

Muesli 24, **25**

muffins

Cruffins Four Ways 218, **219**

Redcurrant Muffins **202**, 204

mushrooms

Portobello Mushrooms, Poached Egg and Hummus on Sourdough **48**, 49

Sesame Tofu with Shiitake Mushroom **120**, 121

Wild Mushroom Soup 80, **81**

Wild Mushroom, Beetroot and Goat's Cheese Tart 182, **183**

Mutaki (Walnut Rolls) **196**, 197

nectarines 108

Noodles, Glass **106**, 107

nuts *9*, 107, 136, 158, 231

Chocolate and Walnut Marble Cake **200**, 201

Walnut Rolls (Mutaki) **196**, 197

oats 24, 27, 43

Octopus with Spaghetti and Romesco Sauce **146**, 147

olive oil *10–11*, 181

Olive and Herbed Provence Bread **226**, 227

omelette 132

with Roasted Asparagus 58, **59**

Onions, Pomegranate 150, **151**

'Our Healthy Breakfast Plate' **70**, 71

Papaya Salad 94, **95**

passionfruit 243, 248

Meringue Tart **210**, 211

pastry

Chudu **232**, 233

Mixed Berry Pie 192, **193**

Strudel **172**, 173

tarts 182, 191, 208, 211

peaches 244

Banana & Peach Waffles **34**, 35

Roast Pork with Fresh Peaches and Thyme 154, **155**

peanuts 107

pecans 24

Roasted Beetroot, Pecan and Feta Salad **96**, 97

peppers 86, 17, 166

Red Pepper Relish 166, **167**

Romesco Sauce **146**, 147

Physalis and Yoghurt Loaf Cake **203**, 205

Pie, Mixed Berry 192, **193**

Pikelets with Blueberries 32, **33**

pineapple 150, 243

pineapple guava *see* feijoa

pitta bread 93

Plums, Beef Stew with Mint and **142**, 143

Poached Chicken and Stracchino Salad 76, **77**

Poached Spiced Quince **30**, 31

Polenta, Herbed Lentils with 68, **69**

pomegranate
    Duck with Quinoa and Pomegranate **152**, 153
    Fig, Walnut, Prosciutto and Pomegranate Salad
        110, 111
    Pomegranate Onions 150, **151**
pork
    Pulled Pork Sliders with a Light Cabbage-Slaw **168**,
        169
    Roast Pork with Fresh Peaches and Thyme 154,
        155
    Slow Roasted Pork with Pineapple and Banana
        Leaves 150, **151**
Portobello Mushrooms, Poached Eggs on Hummus on
    Sourdough **48**, 49
potatoes 90
    Rosemary Potatoes 108, **109**
    Sweet Potato Hummus **130**, 131
prawns 94
    and Scallop Skewers **180**, 181
prosciutto 111
Provence Bread **226**, 227
Pulled Pork Sliders with a Light Cabbage-Slaw **168**,
    169
pumpkins 101
    and Goat's Cheese Savoury Strudel **172**, 173

Quail with Radicchio and Golden Raisins **118**, 119
quinces
    Poached Spiced Quince **30**, 31
    Roast Guinea Fowl with Quince 122, **123**
Quinoa and Pomegranate, Duck with **152**, 153

Radicchio and Golden Raisins, Quail **118**, 119
radishes 55
raisins 140, 158
    Quail with Radicchio and Golden Raisins **118**, 119
    Raisin and Buttermilk Buns 234, **235**
    Spelt, Walnut, Raisin and Fig Bread **229**, 231
Raspberry Tart **190**, 191
Red Salsa 50, **51**
redcurrants
    Chicken with Chestnuts and Redcurrants 136, **137**
    Muffins **202**, 204
Relish, Red Pepper 166, **167**
rice
    with Cranberries 140, **141**
    Cuttlefish with Rice and Tomatoes 148, **149**
    Kale and Aubergine Salad **85**, 87
ricotta 66, 125
roasted meat 122, 154, 157
roasted vegetables 90, 97
Romesco Sauce **146**, 147
rosemary *14*, 108
rye bread **226**, **227**, **228**, 230

salads 76, 79, 107, 108, 119, 153 *see also* dressings,
salad
    Asparagus and Halloumi Salad **84**, 86
    Beetroot Salad with Yuzu Dressing 102, **103**
    Black Rice, Kale and Aubergine Salad **85**, 87
    Cauliflower and Tahini Salad 92, **93**
    Crayfish Salad **98**, 100
    Fig, Walnut, Prosciutto and Pomegranate Salad
        110, 111
    Green Papaya Salad 94, **95**
    Roasted Beetroot, Pecan and Feta Salad **96**, 97
    Ultimate Salad Sandwich 170, **171**
    Watermelon and Feta Salad 88, **89**
salmon
    Dill-Cured Salmon 62, **63**
    and Fennel with Horseradish Spread **53**, 55
    Fillets with Sweet Potato Hummus **130**, 131
salsas
    Avocado and Tomato Salsa 178, **179**
    Caper, Lemon and Olive Oil Salsa **180**, 181
    Mango Salsa **174**, 176
    Skirt Steak with Chimichurri Sauce and Salsa **138**,
        139
    Soft-Fried Eggs with Green and Red Salsa 50, **51**
sandwiches
    Chicken Sandwich with Mango and Avocado **174**, 176
    Lobster Rolls 184, **185**
    Pulled Pork Sliders with a Light Cabbage-Slaw **168**,
        169
    Steak Sandwich with Red Pepper Relish 166, **167**
    Ultimate Salad Sandwich 170, **171**
sauces 169
    Agedashi Sauce **120**, 121
    Chimichurri Sauce **138**, 139
    Romesco Sauce **146**, 147
Scallop and Prawn Skewers **180**, 181
Seared Tuna Salad **78**, 79
seeds *9*, 43, 79, 121
    Three-Seed Rye Bread **228**, 230
Sesame Tofu with Shiitake Mushroom **120**, 121
shellfish 94
    Crab Bruschetta **65**, 67
    Crayfish Salad **98**, 100
    Cuttlefish with Rice and Tomatoes 148, **149**
    Lobster Rolls 184, **185**
    Octopus with Spaghetti and Romesco Sauce **146**,
        147
    Prawn & Scallop Skewers **180**, 181
skewers 177, 181
Skirt Steaks with Chimichurri Sauce and Salsa **138**,
    139
Slaw **168**, 169
Slow Roasted Pork with Pineapple and Banana Leaves
    150, **151**

Slow-Roasted Leg of Lamb with Rainbow Carrots and Herb Yoghurt **160**, 161
smoothies **246–7**, 248–9
Snapper with Walnut, Hazelnut and Raisin Stuffing 158, **159**
Soft-Baked Eggs with Kale and Chorizo **60**, 61
Soft-Fried Eggs with Green and Red Salsa 50, **51**
soups
    Fragrant Butternut Squash Soup **99**, 101
    Roasted Tomato Soup with Sweet Potatoes 90, **91**
    Wild Mushroom Soup 80, **81**
sourdough 49, 66, 67, 166
    Sourdough Bread **224**, 225
Spaghetti, Octopus with **146**, 147
Spelt, Walnut, Raisin and Fig Bread **229**, 231
Spiced Steak Fajitas with Tomato and Avocado Salsa 178, **179**
Steak Sandwich with Red Pepper Relish 166, **167**
Stew, Beef **142**, 143
strawberries 243
    Cheesecake Stuffed Strawberries 214, **215**
Strudel, Pumpkin & Goat's Cheese Savoury **172**, 173
stuffings 148, 158
    Cheesecake Stuffed Strawberries 214, **215**
    Stuffed Baked Tomatoes 144, **145**
    Stuffed Courgette Flowers **124**, 125
Summer Raspberry Tart **190**, 191

tahini *see also* hummus
    Cauliflower and Tahini Salad **92**, 93
tarts
    Fig Tart 208, **209**
    Passionfruit Meringue Tart **210**, 211
    Summer Raspberry Tart **190**, 191
    Wild Mushroom, Beetroot and Goat's Cheese Tart 182, **183**
Three-Seed Rye Bread **228**, 230
thyme *12*, 154
Tofu, Sesame **120**, 121
tomatoes
    and Avocado Salsa 178, **179**
    Cuttlefish with Rice and Tomatoes 148, **149**
    Grilled Herby Lamb with Baby Cherry Tomatoes 116, **117**
    Herbed Lentils with Grilled Polenta and Roasted Tomatoes 68, **69**
    Octopus with Spaghetti and Romesco Sauce **146**, 147
    Roasted Tomato Soup with Sweet Potatoes 90, **91**
    Stuffed Baked Tomatoes 144, **145**
Trout Salad 108, **109**
Truffle Dressing **152**, 153
tuna
    Seared Tuna Salad **78**, 79

Tuna Ceviche on Lettuce Leaves **82**, 83

Ultimate Salad Sandwich 170, **171**

Vanilla and Peach Water 244, **245**
Veggie Garden (juice) **240**, 242

Waffles, Banana & Peach **34**, 35
walnuts 132, 158
    Chocolate and Walnut Marble Cake **200**, 201
    Fig, Walnut, Prosciutto and Pomegranate Salad **110**, 111
    Rolls (Mutaki) **196**, 197
    Spelt, Walnut, Raisin and Fig Bread **229**, 231
Warm Smoked Rainbow Trout Salad 108, **109**
Water, Healthy Vitamin 244, **245**
watermelon 243
    Watermelon and Feta Salad 88, **89**
Wild Mushroom Soup 80, **81**
Wild Mushroom, Beetroot and Goat's Cheese Tart 182, **183**
Wild Rice with Cranberries 140, **141**

yoghurt 36
    Avocado Yoghurt 150, **151**
    Caramelised Figs with Yoghurt **38**, 39
    Herb Yoghurt **52**, 54, **160**, 161
    Physalis and Yoghurt Loaf Cake **203**, 205
Yuzu Dressing 102, **103**

Published in 2016 by
Unicorn, an imprint of Unicorn Publishing Group LLP
101 Wardour Street
London
W1F 0UG
www.unicornpublishing.org

ISBN 978-190787-53-3

10 9 8 7 6 5 4 3 2 1

Project Director: Lucy Duckworth
Designer: Felicity Price-Smith
Indexer: Elizabeth Wise
Photography: Toby Scott
Food Stylist: Maud Eden
Prop Stylist: Sarah Birks
Prop HIre: Daisy Copper ceramics www.daisycooperceramics.com
        Mud Australia www.mudaustralia.com